Don't Think Like a Human!
Channeled answers to basic questions

Kryon
Book II

id you ever dream of sitting at the feet of an angel or a great master and asking about everything? ... Well this is it. In the first book Kryon told a great deal about how things work, and what all the new energies mean for us, but I have so many other basic questions... and so do the readers of Book One.

I can't waste this opportunity to ask more, and you can share in the answers as questions are asked originating from myself and selected readers. That's the subject of this book.

Don't Think Like a Human!
Channeled answers to basic questions
Kryon Book II

Publisher: **The Kryon Writings**

1155 Camino Del Mar – #422
Del Mar, California 92014

Kryon books and tapes can be purchased in
retail stores, or by phone. Credit cards welcome.
(800) 352-6657

Written by Lee Carroll
Proofing/editing by Luana Ewing
Copyright © 1994 Library of Congress
Printed in the United States of America
First Printing September 1994
Second Printing October 1994
Third Printing February 1995
Fourth Printing July 1995
Fifth Printing January 1996 - Revised

ISBN# 0-9636304-0-7 : $12.00 U.S.A.

Table of Contents

continued...

Table of Contents... continued

Foreword...

Kryon's first book, The End Times, introduced us to the concept of Earth alignment, and Kryon's role in the alignment in the past and present. This is Kryon's fourth visit to Earth, and again his function is to make the alignment adjustment the final one before planetary graduation. This is where we come in. We caused a change in the plan, an unexpected change that was not expected.

We are given a gift when a source such as Kryon communicates with us. That is possible because Lee Carroll allowed this to happen in his life and because Jan Tober, his wife, pushed him (gently) until it did happen. Spirit works remarkably!

I have featured Kryon in several issues of Connecting Link magazine, and will continue to do so. His words are vital and important.

Read now, and let yourself expand into the energy that Kryon is. Let him honor you for the work _you_ have done here "in lesson." And let Kryon, who is "in service," be your teacher now for a period of time. Explore your dreams. Read the answers to the questions you have asked. Feel the Love.

Susanne Konicov
Publisher / Editor
Connecting Link magazine

What the Critics said...
About Kryon Book I

"Tired of the 'doom and gloom' predictions of our end times? This newly channeled work is the first book of a series that brings startling positive information that is clear and practical. Packed with life changing potential, it reflects the incredible love of Spirit for humans at this time".

Arizona Networking News
Arizona

"The peaceful loving message that The End Times brings makes fascinating, heartwarming reading."

Leading Edge Review
Minnesota

"I approached Kryon - The End Times with as open a mind as possible and found that I could not put it down. The words of Kryon are loving, peaceful and reassuring. There is a lot of great news."

The Light Connection
California

"What makes Kryon - The End Times remarkable is the fact that the channel had no preestablished beliefs in, nor had he ever studied, Metaphysics. Equally remarkable is the clarity of the information and the loving manner in which it is offered."

The Connecting Link
Michigan

"This book should move well throughout the community since it handles some really big issues in a direct and loving way."

The New Times
Washington

Preface

From the Writer

Kryon Channeling

Don't Think Like a Human!
Book II

From the writer...

I want to encourage anyone reading this now to seek out Kryon Book One. Although all of the Kryon information is interesting and enlightening, it follows a natural sequence of learning and understanding that was presented carefully in suitable order. I believe it would serve you better to find and read book one if you have not. If you do, it will help you in what is to follow.

As I mentioned in Book One, I am a very practical pragmatic person. As a businessman, I spend most of my time in front of computer screens dealing with numbers, planning correspondence and the like. I am not prone to being flighty, and I am very, very skeptical of everything I cannot touch and feel. This kept me away from reading any metaphysical books whatsoever, and never found me at meetings where folks were meditating in groups, waiting for tables to rise or spoons to bend. When Kryon entered my life, there was great cosmic humor over this fact, and now I understand why.

The Universe needed someone with an open heart and an empty mind... and boy did it find one! The cosmic humor results in the fact that I contracted to do this before I ever came in; but of course I do not know this while I am here. I represent the attitude of countless humans who would never be caught dead in a séance, unless of course they were dead and attending in that form (Earth humor). And so I remain the proverbial doubting Thomas, even as I continue to channel this great loving entity called Kryon.

This is as it should be, for it serves me well to be this way. It not only keeps me honest, but it keeps things happening with a degree of integrity toward this process that otherwise might be simply accepted as par for the course. My feelings are that this experience is hardly "par.".... and I have yet to locate the course.

Here's what I do know: Since Kryon Book One was released, amazing things have happened to me and those around me. The book was read and accepted by workers and nonworkers alike. I received countless letters from all over the Northern Hemisphere! Many sought me out and wanted a closer look. I sat with individuals and groups and just let the information and love flow... and it has made a difference in many lives.

I learned how to communicate with my guides, and found them receptive... to the extent that I actually felt I was creating my own reality. I would explain things, and ask for help creating action... and would get it sometimes within one day! This is powerful stuff. I took my new power and am continuing to work with it daily; then I discovered how logical it was too!

How can I explain how my heart feels? I have unwarranted peace, "too peaceful for what I know is going on around me." This is an actual statement, and may sound like I need psychological help, but it is literal. I feel better than I should under circumstances that heretofore would normally have produced less peace, or even anxiety. And that's not all... I'm starting to feel balanced for the first time in my life. I view others differently, and often my heart overflows with love for them. At the same time I see appropriateness in all things, even death. My tolerance level has zoomed! Those about whom I loved to complain have simply become other precious humans in lesson, and I actually found myself understanding what they were going through. The things they did that previously drove me nuts no longer pushed any of my buttons. I found myself giving thought energy to helping them! What a shift in purpose! And the wild thing is that it's working.

Some say it's a massive desensitization process, a turn inward to the extent of ignoring everything around you... the ostrich syndrome. To me it is exactly the opposite: it is an outreach in love that encompasses full understanding of universal principles, creating greater wisdom for reaction while in lesson, opening the door to healing and actually changing the future for our planet. This sounds a bit grandiose, I know, but it's the direction of things to come, and it feels so natural.

Why do I tell you all this? Because I find myself in a strange dichotomy of mind. I continue to experience the unseen, heretofore weird "unreal" forces as I move into this new era of my life, comfortable with all of it since it is actually happening, and not imagined. And yet I remain with many questions about "how come?"

I have a much broader base to work from now that Kryon has done so much explanation of how things work for us, and I have experienced "cause-and-effect" as proof that it is accurate. But I still have many, many questions about what I see around me.

I have decided to proceed in this book to ask my partner (Kryon) the hard questions that I have about many of the things that seem odd to me, or intangible. Why is it this way? What do we make of such and such? Who are these other entities around? Many readers also have written to ask related questions about the first book, and I will ask some of those also.

Prepare yourself. I'm going to ask some "doozies," because this subject is too important not to. As before, I write this prior to the channeling, so that you and I both can share in the information at the same time.

Chapter One

About Love

About Love
Chapter One

Greetings! I am Kryon of magnetic service. Before I allow questions to proceed, I wish to reacquaint you with my energy, and bring you closer to the vibration of my partner who is currently channeling these words.

I am of magnetic service, and exist solely for the purpose of service to you – who are dearly loved and exalted among entities. You are the ones in lesson, and you are the ones who are the special ones walking on this planet. I am here to respond to your works, which have been significant in the past 50 years. You have changed your future... and you are poised at a place now where you can do it again. Believe me, the entire Universe knows of the situation you call planet Earth. With my changes, you can have increased power... and this is why I have allowed communication – so that you will understand what to do next.

My partner admonished you to complete the previous communications. These are critical for your growth and explain a great deal about why I am here, and what is currently happening. It will serve you well to seek out the first series if you have not yet seen it.

Dear one, if you think you have picked up this book by accident, then you really do not understand how things work. For

I am Kryon, and know you... and you know me. If these words, or those of past writings seemed to feel like "home" to you, then it is because your higher self has intuitively recognized the writing of a friend. I love you dearly, as do all entities who are here in service like the Kryon. I admonish you to let yourself feel my presence in your heart, and let yourself have the peace which can be yours when you let go of the fear that prevails even now in most humans.

The ancients told you that "the meek will inherit the planet." Unfortunately your word "meek" was a poor choice for translation. Indeed the meek will inherit the planet, but you should be aware of what meek really means. The meek human is submissive to the power of love. That is, a meek person chooses to stand back in wisdom when others charge in with anger. A meek person will choose to evaluate another in the criterion of love rather than of wealth, position or situation. A meek person is truly without ego, and is slow to defend himself, even when verbally attacked. This is because a meek person has the wisdom to understand that a verbal attack harms nothing, and is the result of imbalance in the attacker. A meek person will send love to those who attack, and regularly feature balance toward the Earth, with tolerance even toward the intolerable.

Who is this meek person? This meek person is among the most powerful on the planet. This meek person is the one who has recognized love as the power source, and creates with it. She or he changes negative to positive and evil to kindness. This person has the power to heal individuals, and groups of these people can change the planet itself. All warriors will pale in comparison to this meek person, for the power of one of these balanced ones will be equal to legions of those without love.

I come to you representing this power, and with the news that it can finally be yours. This powerful meek person is you. Put away your fears of the phantoms of lesson and claim this power. I will support you with my changes, and your guides will give you what you need to continue. Understand who you are! Understand who you are! Understand who you are! *(There is no greater emphasis than when Kryon repeats something three times.)*

Love is the champion of the times. It is the bond of the Universe, and is the secret of your unified theory. It is present at the cellular level, ready to be released with appropriate action. It is unconditional, and is unique. It provides peace where none existed before. It provides rest where none was possible before. It is wise. It is the sun within the sun, and is of singular source. There is nothing greater than this. No evil or negative thing can compare to it, and it is yours for the taking in the new energy.

Know this my friend: you cannot undo this truth of what you are reading now. It will stick in your consciousness long after you put down this book. It rings of truth because it is. Claim it!

Kryon

Chapter Two

Questions
The Confusion

Questions
"The Confusion"
Chapter Two

Question: Kryon, I honor your presence and your love, and I recognize the feelings of having you with me now, as always. You have brought me to this point of wanting to know more about the way things work, and so I will ask several multifaceted questions, in the same way you have given multifaceted answers in the past. Let me begin with a very basic one:

I was in a metaphysical store the other day, and was bewildered by the seeming conglomeration of diverse systems and methods, all staring at me from the shelves. To name a few, there were books and advice from many different strange sounding (and looking) yogis and teachers. There were books and methods on Astrology, tarot, rebirthing, past-life regression, psychic surgery and UFOs... all on the same shelf! There were rocks and gems for sale that were supposed to mean something, or heal something. There were runes and books for the meaning of runes. There were methods on color healing, sound healing, aroma healing, and touch healing. There were books of patterns and colors that supposedly were significant. There were star histories, star charts, fixed star charts, solar charts and moon phase charts. There was information on auras, chakras, meditation methods and even human spiritual sex. Then I swallowed really hard when I noticed the "channeling section...". It seemed there were endless entities doing exactly what I am doing now, with rows of books. It continued with books about the Earth ancients, and books from the American Indians, and books even from space!

What does this all mean? How can we make our way within this seemingly competing hodgepodge of information? Which one is correct? How can we choose?

Answer: Greetings! Again, I speak to all of you now with an even clearer voice than before, due to my partner's experience with my ongoing work.

Throughout these answers you will read a recurring theme. It is about your culture, your imprints, and the assumptions that they breed within your way of thinking. In past writings I spoke of your Earth religion, and how it has been tempered and shaped to suit men's needs for control. There is no greater example of this than the posture of your (*my partner's*) question.

All of you have been taught from birth about giving your power away to God, and becoming submissive and subservient. You worship by bowing and groveling and crawling before a Godhead because of your self-taught unworthiness as a human. You continue to search for the one God, the one system, or the one doctrine that explains everything to your satisfaction. This doctrine usually ends up being a set of rules or methods to gain God's favor, or to clearly explain a simple cause-and-effect relationship regarding punishment or reward.

Dear one, when you walked through the store, who informed you that you were to choose a religion from the shelf? This was not a place with competing doctrines asking you to "choose" one, or embrace a belief. Let me ask you this: when you were in school as a young person, which subject did you "believe in"? Which one did you accept while casting off the others? Was it science, or history, or trade workshop, or language? This is a silly question (you might say)... well indeed! You were in school as a young eager <u>empowered</u> human ready to learn about your world and your work, and the training thereof. It never entered your mind to choose a subject, let it subjugate you and cast off the others.

So it is now with you spiritually. Let me be very clear on this. The store you were in is the "hardware store" of the mechanical universal ways of things. In there you could have found the parts and pieces of all the knowledge you have yet amassed regarding the way things work for an empowered "piece of God" walking on this planet. As I will continue to remind you, you are the special ones. You are the empowered ones, and you are the ones I am here to serve. There are no greater entities on this Earth than the ones in lesson! Believe it! All the others are here to service your stay here. This knowledge is blocked from you, and hidden in your phantom reality of lesson, but it is true nonetheless. Your duality is your area of discovery.

The combined shelves are your encyclopedias for knowledge. All the things you spoke of have appropriateness... all of them! Yes, there is healing in stones, and in colors, and in sounds, and in patterns. As I informed you earlier, the real power will be to the few who finally put them together! For now, even apart they are still valid. Are humans being healed with these? The answer is YES. There is appropriateness in Astrology, which is the study of the magnetic alignment of your birth imprint. There is real value in learning about Tarot and Rune methods. These are thermometers of your growth at the moment, and really do reflect accuracy at the highest level when used and interpreted correctly. There is much to know, if you desire, about how your body is physically balanced; thus the study of auras and chakras and even human spiritual sex. Sex was not given to you simply as a biological way of procreation. It was also meant to be a spiritual bridge between the female and male, bonding spiritually while at the same time providing the necessary biological functions.

Books from the ancients, or the yogis and shamans, are your time capsules from yourselves to yourselves... did this never occur to you? Perhaps this will give you a brand new perspective about history. What part do you think you played in it? Could any of these on the shelves of the ancients be you? Surely you find this intriguing. This is something I can not experience as the Kryon. It is yours alone, and it is revealing in its truth. Buried in your past expressions are wonderful pointers as to why you are the way you are today. Also, the way you are today will affect your next expression as well. These are complex but wonderful mechanics of your lessons in karma, and you should desire to know more about it, for it will serve you immediately.

As for the variety of authors, be aware that the truth is the truth, and you will find cohering principles at every step, even though the cultures and languages differ.

The channeled books? I know you will have more questions on this. Most are real. Some are not. Your intuition will give you the truth. The ones that are real have been channeled at the highest level by vastly different entities of service and teaching; that is why the information is so diverse. It is not necessarily opposing, just differing in perspectives. I will give you more on this later, but I will tell you, as I have before, that channeled predictions are not all accurate due to the changing of the Earth in the last years. It might have been accurate for the time it was written, but not necessarily now. However, some predictions of over 1,000 years ago are again accurate, having been rendered void through human action, and then returned to accuracy recently. Does this surprise you? Remember that you have a limited linear time line, and the Universe does not. All real channeled information is always given in perfect love energy. I don't have to explain to you, my partner, how this affects the outcome, do I? As far as a channeling from space... what do you think this is?

I also have given you insight in the last writings about UFOs. Is it any wonder that they play such an important part in Metaphysics? Remember the admonition: things not yet understood are not necessarily evil, weird, or spooky... just not yet understood. Give these things space and tolerance as you would if you suddenly discovered a brand new physical law to study (which by the way, you will).

For all of you, the next time you approach these stores, do so with love and tolerance. Then describe verbally to each other how you feel. Which books do you reach for? What do you wish to know more about? As an entity of divine origin, walking the planet in lesson, what do you wish to know? ... Then pick the appropriate material. Your gift of discernment is especially keen in this new energy. It won't be long before the wheat is separated from the chaff regarding the shelves of these stores.

Question: You said, "Your duality is your area of discovery." What does this mean? I have heard others speak of the "duality." What is it?

Answer: This is a difficult concept for you to realize. It's difficult since it is purposefully blocked to every human in lesson. In previous writings I have spoken about it over and over, and even yet it is a seeming puzzle to you. It's time for you to put away the old ways of thinking and embrace the new basic truths.

Please be clear and understand the following: you are all high entities walking on this planet, disguised as simple biological beings... and the disguise fools everyone, even you. This is the basis of the duality. You are really two people. The "real you" is the high entity, whose power and knowledge each of you owns, and the "phantom" is the shell of humanism in lesson. The irony here is that you perceive the phantom as real, and the real you as the phantom. Many of you don't perceive the real one at all! The biggest discoveries in lesson that you will make are concerning this duality. The biggest successes you will have in growth are based in understanding how the duality works, and finally gaining realization of the reversed "real" and "phantom" roles. Although you cannot truly see your higher self (for that would void the purpose of your lesson), you can gain a working knowledge and understanding of the reality of who you are. When this occurs, then you can take your power... and not before. Therefore your area of discovery is that of self-awareness and the truth of the duality within you, and how to enhance it.

Also I can never state this enough: you and those around you selected your human circumstances well before you ever arrived. The things you are going through right now are part of a plan set in motion by you. Please do not confuse this with predestination. Predestination plays no part in this at all. True predestination creates problems and dictates solutions. In the present situation, you have given yourselves only the problems. The solutions happen through your self-awareness and realization. You are given a problem and the tools and power to work it out. When you do, this in turn raises the vibration of the planet.

Question: How is it that our personal self-realization, and our personal working through lesson, creates a planetary vibration change. That seems a bit grandiose. Why doesn't it only affect us individually?

Answer: This is a simple answer. In past writings I spoke of the importance between you personally and the Earth as a whole. I am here doing something for the Earth, but it directly translates to your spiritual power and health. The planet is the classroom. You are within it, and everything that happens to the classroom happens to you. The reverse is also true. The more enlightenment exists, the more the planet is balanced.

Eventually the classroom is filled with knowledgeable students, and isn't needed when the students graduate. During the process from learning to graduation, the classroom is slowly changed as there are more and more students who pass their lessons. Even when you were in school, isn't it true that you could walk into a classroom and tell what grade level was being taught? Didn't that tell you also what level the students were at? The classroom changes as the learning grows. Old lessons are discarded, and newer, more advanced ones are presented. The whole changes with the parts, and the parts define the change.

The other reason is that you (as the parts) are not really alone in your lesson. You have significant inner workings with others around you (by design and agreement beforehand). Therefore what you perceive to be personal growth changes the group in the same way it changes the classroom.

Question: I want to ask you more about the way this group karma works later, but right now I wish to start a dialogue about psychics and channels. First off: who am I that I should be doing this? If the answer seems to be self-serving or personal, I'll understand it's only for me, and I won't include it in the book.

Answer: The answer is hardly self-serving; it's simple truth! You agreed to do this prior to your coming. Now is the chosen time... and here you are. There isn't much more than that. Much of what you have done during your life has prepared you for this, as was the plan. Your interest in the logical wasn't an accident, nor was the fact that you embraced fundamental Christian beliefs early on. This kept you well clear of Metaphysics, but still within the love vibration. This made for a perfect "bed" to allow for good trans-lations, clear of bias. If anything, you are biased toward the practical and logical, and that brings us to why you are asking the questions that you are now.

Question: Why don't I leave my body during channeling like the others? It seems far less dramatic for those who attend the Kryon sessions. And without going into "trance," how can I know that the things I am translating are accurate?

Answer: One of the attributes of the new energy is responsibility and integrity. You will start to notice that channels no longer have to "give away" their own personality to that of the entity delivering the message. Clearer messages will be able to be given now that you are carrying the whole power of your own soul. The best channeling is a partnership; before it was a "takeover." It had to be, since you could not contain a situation which comingled that kind of power with your old vibration. With the new partnership comes full integrity. This is not to say that there was no integrity before. Hardly! But before, a channel could "turn it over" and resign the information and actions as coming from someone else. Now the partnership demands that responsibility is taken by the one in lesson as well, since he is an active participant. The new clearing of interpretation is actually caused by the fact that your "higher self" (which knows everything I know) verifies the translation before you put it out. This is the integrity check. This is new. This new method is more difficult than the old way, since it involves your human personality as totally aware during channeling. It is more difficult in the fact that you must practice staying "inside" yourself during channeling, and it is imperative that ego be sublimated.

Those who are most comfortable with the old method of channeling can continue in full harmony with what is happening now, but the new energy will bring a better, clearer method to use if desired.

Question: Why do some feel that a channel has to huff and puff, or speak in a strange voice in order to be believed? Why do some in attendance even wish to be "spoken down" to, like children? How does this serve them?

Answer: Do not judge any individual, channel or attendee! All is appropriate for the time. Many must have a simulated authority figure in front of them, with all the attributes of a parent, in order to feel that there is validity. Some must have the drama of what they perceive as an off-world figure to feel the credibility of the channel. Would you take any of this away, and lose the precious-ness of self-discovery for these? The work of these other channels is every bit as valid as your own. Think carefully before you verbalize criticism of anyone else's way of accepting Spirit! Dear partner, in love... stand admonished for this question.

Question: I must ask another sensitive question that has always bothered me. Why it is that psychics and channels seem to never quite "line up" with each other in what they see or predict? How can this be if they are all "reading" the same universe?

Answer: This isn't a difficult question, or an improper one... but again, your perception of what to expect taints your reactions. Let's be clear on this: if you could see your full soul, and know what was on the other side of the veil, then there would be no need for your lesson here. Follow this reasoning and realize that your knowledge and perceptions about the "other side" are gleaned through filters of thought and intuition, and are rarely given to you in a form that is conclusive. Picture this: if you could all get together and prove absolutely that you were a piece of God walking the Earth in lesson... in disguise, then we (*the Universe*) would "turn on the lights" and you would all go home! Class dismissed.

As for interpretations and predictions, you still continue to see through the darkened glass... except that many of you are realizing that the glass has been clearing up lately, allowing much clearer translations. Let me give you a new perception on psychics and "see-ers." Let's say that three psychics were desiring to see what was on the other side of a door (*in this case the door represents the veil*). They couldn't open the door since that was not per-mitted. Instead, they discovered that if they knelt down, they had the ability that some others did not of seeing through the space under the door. All three kneel down and peer under the door. All three are shown the same thing through the crack: they see another smaller door, and the lower part of some shoes. All of them are shown this identical picture, but now there is much to extrapolate from the picture.

All the psychics are seeing 100 percent accuracy, and at this point they are all given a true and accurate glimpse of the other side. This is their gift, and they all see what is given as truth. One psychic thinks the smaller door is an opening to your higher self, and that the type of shoes indicates a tall male guide is standing on the other side of the door, ready to help. Another psychic thinks that the smaller door is a locked door, and leads to the cave of knowledge, and that the shoes contain a female angel, standing with the key. The third psychic, who is the most balanced of all, comes to no decision at all until he (1) askes his higher self to verify what he is seeing, and (2) if in doubt, consults with others of like mind for their opinion. Why consult with others? Because the new energy promotes this. There is added power and clarity with combined efforts now.

After verification the third psychic is far more able to translate, since he is able to abolish human assumption, which often gets in the way. He finds that the shoes are only shoes, without anyone standing in them at all. It was a poor Earth assumption on the part of the others that concluded that all shoes have an entity wearing them. The door? The balanced psychic realized that it is only a mirror, reflecting the back side of the door he is looking under. It won't open at all; it's an illusion. Not all things open that look like doors. He then goes on to translate the meaning of a pair of shoes and the reflected door, something that would have escaped the others altogether. Therefore, you had three valid psychics who all saw the truth, but only one knew what it really was. This calls upon wisdom, balance, and discernment from the human. A good psychic in the new energy has two talents: the first of being able to "see" under the door, the second, the ability to discern what it all means. This is exactly what happened with the false predictions about the Earth's tilt. As stated before in earlier writings, the tilt is magnetic only, and is my job. The idea of the shift was accurately "seen" by many, but not fully understood by all.

The Universe is quite literal. All is not what it seems from your side, even if you think you may have the answer to a mystery. You first must abolish all Earth-based assumptions. This is basically what is wrong with your scientific method at the moment. I will give you more on this in the future if you wish, but suffice it to know that you cannot discern physical universal truths if you apply human precepts and assumptions to your logic models.

So you see, there is much truth to be gleaned... such as you are receiving now; but you must put your cultural and Earth-based assumptions aside. Now you can freely translate even things which don't seem to make sense within your old logic patterns, but which will someday be commonplace knowledge.

Kryon

Chapter Three

Personalities
in Channelings

Personalities in Channelings
Chapter Three

B
efore you ask more about the channels who interest you, here is more information about what has recently taken place on Earth regarding such things. It may be interesting for you to note that most of your channelled information of the past has come through entities who have been in lesson on Earth, and have come back with information for you. This will not change, and as I have said, it is still appropriate. You may verify this easily by asking the channeled entity directly. They all have names. Some of the names are the ones they had in lesson, while others are using their sound tone names (or as close to it as they can in your hearing... like I am doing). Almost all of them will willingly admit who they were while on Earth.

There are two reasons why these channels are beneficial: The first is that they have been through lesson on your planet, and are fully aware of the experience, and can relate to your own lessons and phantoms. They have experienced the duality, and have resided in bodies like your own. This gives them a wonderful platform of knowledge to work from, for they already know what you are feeling when they work with you. The second reason that a former "lesson channel" has been appropriate is that these were the only entities who could withstand the lower vibratory rate of your bodies in these past times. Without the new energy and new adjustments and "permission" given by your works, there could be none of the type as the Kryon. This simply means that they had to be in lesson at least once in order to return and channel through a human. Now, in the new energy you get the advantage of both kinds of channels. The new energy opens up the information flow for <u>both</u> kinds, even those who have been channeling with you for years.

Let me explain that for the first time the Kryon and others like me are now free to be with you, channeling while you are in lesson. This is new, and you have won this appropriately. Now you can have entities giving you information that are in service only, never having been in lesson anywhere in the Universe. Our purpose is to bring you new information that the others were not allowed to give in the old energy, and to bring you a new scope of understanding. As stated, the others are also allowed this now, but don't be surprised if some of the others appropriately leave and actually go on to be in lesson again... having finished their work in channel. This is a clue to their service: that is, to experience lesson around the Universe, then to return as channeled teachers in the bodies of the types they incarnated in while in lesson.

As I have explained in the other writings, the Kryon has always existed, and my sole purpose is to serve those in lesson as a magnetic master, or better described as a technician in service. I have full knowledge of the workings of the Universe, and have full knowledge of your lesson structure, just like you do when you are not here. Your structure is not that much different from that of the others. Don't be surprised one day when the entity that gets out of a UFO to greet you looks very much like you! There are many variations, of course, but not near to the extent of your imaginative stories.

There are many of us in service, and our service to you varies greatly, as does our information due to our specialty. My specialty is to explain your duality, your magnetic grid importance, your body's reactions to my work, your imprint functions, and your implants. I also can explain anything within appropriateness about your past lives, and the way things work in general. My main goal at this time, however, is to make you aware of the new power you have through the love energy, in order to help you clear yourselves of the phantom fears that still pervade your inner consciousness.

Others of us have vastly different knowledge to give you. Examples are: the Master Teachers, the Master Technicians (like me), the Guides and the Master guides, those in lesson who return as teachers (channels), the Angels (working directly with the singular source), and the vast array of internal workers. There is so much activity and support around you, that you would be astounded! A great deal goes into making this planet of yours work for your lesson. There are great numbers of entities working for each human in lesson.

Are you getting a sense of how special you are? Even as my partner translates this last sentence, I feel within him a twinge of discomfort. I will answer his questions about those now dying on your planet later in this book. Those who are dying are proof of how much the Universe is doing in your arena right now.

You are dearly loved. We are here in all appropriateness and correctness for you, and you alone. You now have the ability to fully understand this, as well as to move forward with much greater power, enlightenment, and wisdom. **To be alive in lesson at this time is because you selected it. It is no accident that you are here now.** Realize this and soar to the place you were made to be in. Make this incarnation one to celebrate!

Kryon

Chapter Four

Questions about
Earth channels

Questions about Earth Channels

Chapter Four

From the writer:

The following are questions about certain personalities that are known to me, that either are channeling on the Earth now, or have given predictions. Even if you are unaware of these people, please read on, for within the body of the answers from Kryon will contain general information of value.

Question: I am curious what you wish to tell me about the one called Ramtha. This entity has a high profile as channeled entities go, and has enjoyed popularity and fame for many years. Is this entity appropriate?

Answer: You should know that there are no inappropriate entities channeling for you on the Earth. If there is inappropriateness, it is within those who are human, pretending to be channels, or those calling on negativity to serve them, feigning the dark side. With Ramtha there is total appropriateness, and good information is being given.

Ramtha, known to me as a three-syllable entity RAM-MA-THA, is of the highest in service. His attributes are almost those of a renegade; but there is no denial or separatism involved, only the freedom. Ramtha is free to serve in a non-structured arena throughout the Universe, whereas I am fully structured, and respond to your lessons. All of this is as it should be. Ramtha is of the kind of service I spoke about earlier. He is an entity who goes through lesson (or several), then comes back to give you whatever he feels you need based on his experience while on your planet. He indeed is a master, and has the freedom of such. His messages are specific for those who need them, as opposed to a general message such as mine. He always teaches from love (as do we all).

Ramtha is a singular channeled entity, and works only through one human individual. This is an old energy concept, and had to be this way... but might face change shortly. He is free to leave anytime he wishes, and when he does, he may decide to revisit in lesson with you or somewhere else in the Universe. This kind of service is very special, as you might imagine, for there is great variety involved, and much knowledge required.

Question: You said that Ramtha was a "singular" channeled entity, and yet Ramtha teaches others how to channel his energy. In Kryon Book One, you also said that the Kryon channels were limited to only nine, but then you said everyone can call on you for help. How does this work?

Answer: It is impossible for me to actually explain the working of this, but I can tell you of the intent, and therefore you can understand the results. This process has many layers. The top one is the single channel of Ramtha, or in my case, the nine humans who are channeling the Kryon on Earth. The other layers are of similar energy, but without the force of the demand for writing and training. Think of the top layer as the original giving of the truth and energy, and the next layers as the sharing of it. All of you can call upon the energy of any entity that has been given appropriate ability and permission to share it. Only a few of you can issue original information with authority and integrity.

Many entities of total service in the new energy can have first-layer multiple human translators. The number is limited to those who have contracts to do so. As already mentioned in previous writings, the Kryon is being translated by nine humans on Earth at this time (*look for the actual areas on Earth as described in Book*

One). It is the same with Solara. This precious entity is also giving messages and teaching worldwide in areas that may never be exposed to the current western writings. It is also possible that none of you will ever meet each other (*those channeling the same entity*).

Also know this, my partner: if you were to have rejected this window of opportunity from the Kryon, I would have moved to the next human in line. These messages are too important to be stopped by the ego of any human in lesson. I congratulate all of you who have seen the windows and walked through them.

Question: The woman who channels Ramtha has been criticized by some for her life-style and her accumulation of wealth during her time of channel. What can you say about that?

Answer: Her evaluation from the Universe is not critical. She is celebrated for having given her life to this quest. Other humans have reacted to her position, and the non-believers will always be intolerant, since they will immediately suspect fraud. Let me ask you this: I have already given you the method for attaining sustenance and abundance while in lesson through good guide communication. I have told you that it is your reward to be able to have peace and lack of worry about such things. Would you then deny some other workers this gift, while you took it for yourself? Also, what would you require in earthly payment if I were to ask you to give up your life-styles and teach for me... and thereby lose part of your remaining years in this lifetime? This human channel has done all of these things, and has obviously been given sustenance and abundance. Approach your attitude about her with the tolerance of love that I have been speaking of. She is dearly loved, and is to be celebrated. Can you see her as I do?

There is great earthly wealth accumulated in almost all of your large religions on Earth, even the ones who serve the hungry and poor. You have come to accept this, so why would it be different for those in other service? The "love" mechanics are the same here, for the Universe is literal, and sees and honors sincere communication without bias, from the one or the many. As discussed earlier, you can see results of prayer all over the planet, and the names humans give to the religion or sect doing the work is meaningless. The key is love. Work and communication done in love will get results; and make no mistake about this: **you deserve to be comfortable and abundant while you are in lesson**. Ramtha is teaching this as well. You will find this theme prevalent in all the new energy teachers, for it is a basic truth.

Question: With so many in poverty and dying on the planet at this time, how can this really be so? It sounds a bit unbelievable.

Answer: It is true that all of you are here to go through karma and the lessons associated with it. This is correct for all parts of the world. You will note that I said that you "deserve" comfort and abundance. Humans who deny the duality, who remain unbalanced, who reject love, who embrace negativity and who choose to repeat and repeat karma will not have comfort or peace until they reverse the process. Those who deserve a reward will not receive it until they step up to the platform and take it.

Dear ones, can you realize now that this message is important that we bring to you? Realize your duality. Realize your power. Realize your lesson, and make steps toward tolerance and love communication to your guides. It is as simple as that. Each of you has a very different situation, but the duality is absolutely universal among humans. This message is for everyone, even those who are starving and dying in the third world. The reason it is being seen first in the West is so that you, who have more comfort, can assemble together and give good verbalization in prayer and meditation for the others. I have already given you the mechanics in the first writings for this. Now use it to help the others.

Question: There is another I am curious about. Tell me about *Solara*. I have not read the channeled books, as you have instructed me not to, but there is strong connection for me here.

Answer: It is no wonder that you "feel" the connection. Solara is of the new energy. This entity, also channeled by a woman, is of the type I described that is in total service. The actual name is far different than "Solara," but it is appropriate for your language, and has some of the same tone attributes that tell who this is. Solara is a gold color to you, much as the Kryon would be a copper color, as described in earlier writings.

There are many semantic differences within channels, depending on their own personal translations. After all, you (*my partner*) are using your own biological brain and cultural education to translate my thought packages. I tell you this because I do not want you, or those reading this, to get confused over the name labels of the universal entities. The label names you give to them – guides, angels, masters, etc. – are unimportant. What is important is their vibration. Is it total love? Then use discernment to evaluate their purpose, and you will have them compartmentalized, as you humans need to do to feel good about them.

Solara is of the highest order. Solara is a master teacher (or angel to some). This entity relates to you (*my partner*), since the "feeling" is the same as mine. The love is overwhelming as this entity speaks through the human who has elected to do the work. It is the same with you, and you feel the same "love wash" that she feels, since our vibrations are very similar.

My service is different and more specific than that of Solara, but we both have very specific attributes in common: we both are service entities only. That is, neither of us have been humans on Earth. Both of us are here in the new energy to give specific education and teaching in love. Neither of us could have been here before now. Solara arrived before I did in all appropriateness to teach you an overview about the way things work. As a master teacher, Solara is allowed to instruct you in star information. This information is given in love, just as my specific information is also given in love about your individual lives. Look closely for the similarities; the love vibration is everywhere. We both speak of the vibrational changes. We both speak of the window of energy change, and your new powers, and we both speak of a new dimension for human thinking and enlightenment. This teacher also foretold my work. Look for it.

Solara also gives the channel the same "overlay" as you (*my partner*) have, something you have never spoken about to anyone. It would be easy for you to become Kryon, and leave your old life behind you. This is the oneness you feel for me, and the necessary way we must exist together for you to do your work.

Question: Three years ago I sat passively in front of Dr. Frank Alper, who channels an entity he calls Adamis. He is the one who first spoke of you by name. Subsequently I have come to respect his reading with me. Tell me about Adamis.

Answer: Adamis is truly a pioneer. What a challenge this entity had... to incarnate, and while on Earth, recognize the duality so completely that it could channel itself while in lesson ... and all this in the old energy as well! This dear one is celebrated constantly at the highest level. Adamis is a very old Earth soul who contracted to spend this incarnation in a role that was a forerunner of things to come. It is fitting that he should do so, since his past life history is so rich in elevating civilization. It is the desire of all of us that each of you would recognize the duality to the degree that you could get information in this manner. If any of you become "one" with your soul while in lesson, you leave immediately and instantly, since the lesson no longer serves you or the planet. What this entity has done, however, is to establish guide communication so seamless with his soul that good, clear translations have resulted... to the benefit of many over the years, including yourself (*my partner*).

In addition, Adamis is here on Earth for the last time. He, like myself, has technical attributes, and will continue service to the Earth until the end. He knows me, and I know him. There is much love here, as well as a great deal of cosmic humor... that one day you will understand.

Question: Finally, what can we make of the predictions of the ancient Nostradamus?

Answer: Nostradamus was hardly an ancient, but in your terminology he was an historic prophet whose predictions seem to have accuracy over the span of four centuries. This is important. Put away his work now. The new energy has voided his sight. He was accurate, but your work in raising the vibration of the planet to the status of the new energy has changed your future. As described for you in past writings, his maps and predictions of your coastlines after 2001, and the maps of the Hopi Indians are different. Even though they were both channeled at the highest level, the Hopi predictions are clearer – even though they were first! All of this represents what I have been speaking of: that the future is a moving target, subject to your work... and your linear time line is a phantom to actual universal reality.

Again, this is why I am here. Your new vibration is your earned situation and your reward for the work you have done raising the planet's energy. Don't believe anyone who tells you exactly what will happen to your planet at a given time. This is all in transition, and is totally up to you to change.

Kryon

Chapter Five

Past Lives
Future Lives

Past Lives – Future Lives
Chapter Five

The fact is that all of you share the circumstance that you have been on Earth many times. I gave explanation in previous writings as to how your many expressions work together as a system, using karma (overlays) and "doors" of action to provide a way for you to work through your incarnations (*The End Times,* Chapter One). You may also recognize that a recurring theme of these translations is how much you are honored for this. I will speak of this over and over, and will continue to do so until it is time for me to leave. I cannot emphasize enough how much you are loved, and how you are celebrated by those of us in service. The reason is simple: you have chosen to be the **warriors of the light**. You are the ones who make the difference and create the change. All the rest of us are in support of you... but <u>you</u> must do the work. Your entire Earth structure, all recorded Earth history, and everything you behold as a human, revolves around this. This is critical work for the Universe. The reasons why this is so important to the Universe will remain veiled for a bit longer, and is not important to you at this time. But you have to know your work is far greater in purpose for us than simply making your planet enlightened. Please believe me when I tell you that!

The overall universal "plan" is to place you in lesson on Earth, with the duality as previously described, and with the tools to make personal change. You are given complex attributes and challenges, and your reaction to those challenges is your work. When the reaction is positive, and you choose to enlighten yourselves and work through them, then you personally and collectively raise the vibration of the planet... which is the goal. If you do not, then you repeat with a heavier overlay.

When you stand on the sidelines ready to go into lesson, you stand as full entities, honored and continually serviced by all of us, equal to any entity with your attributes in the Universe. Anywhere you go you are instantly recognized and honored for your work, for you display the colors or badges of lesson. You draw up the plans together, and then you enter at appropriate times to implement the lesson plan. In this, **you are the architect of your own lesson, and therefore you always have the answers to the lessons within yourself**... hiding in the duality, available almost at any time you choose through self-realization and communication with your soul.

As previously translated, it is my job to create the magnetic balance of the Earth to correspond to your work. Magnetism is the "couch" that human consciousness and biology has been sitting in for its entire existence. It is critical for your balance, and allows for enlightenment. I was here to set up the magnetics prior to your arrival, and I was here two other times since to adjust it. This is my fourth and final time here for the planet as you know it.

It may still seem odd to you that you have been here over and over. This fact is very well suppressed by your imprint at birth, and that is why it remains controversial to this day within the circles of spiritual leadership. This is as it should be, however, for to have it otherwise would not serve the purpose of the duality. You each have full knowledge of all your incarnations, for your soul entity knows all of them. Your soul entity also carries around the lesson plan (while it is on Earth), the past history, and the answers for you to graduate! If this is so (you might ask), then why don't you just ask yourself about it? Indeed! That is the entire quest. Obtaining enlightenment to get to the place where you realize you can ask is 90% of the work. Asking for the knowledge is only the last 10%. All of you can access knowledge of past lives and use the knowledge to clear karma. This was put in place as a method for you, and is provided as a way to help you with peace in your current situation.

There are several ways to clear karmic attributes. When you do clear them, you are given an implant to neutralize the part of your imprint that assigned the karma to you in the first place. (1) One way to clear karma is the oldest and most painful: it is the "go through it" method. This quite often requires a lifetime sacrifice and sometimes termination (death). (2) Another way is through the realization that it exists. This can only come through enlightenment. When you are at a place of balance, many times the karmic lesson is revealed to you through intuition or dreams, or even through singular distress situations that suddenly "clear" things for you. Once you realize and recognize the karmic attribute, then it is almost void. You must then face it firmly and identify it completely in order to void it. Think of it as searching in tall grass for remedies to certain aches and pains you have. Once you discover the remedy, you apply it to your body to clear the pain for that specific item. Then you continue to search the grass for the next remedy, until all pain is gone.

(3) Another way to clear a karmic attribute is related to the last, but with added help from another balanced human. As previously translated, you cannot easily help yourself if you are not balanced, and sometimes it takes others to bring you to that state so that you can then continue to heal yourself. This is why it is appropriate for those called facilitators to continue working with you. Even in the new energy these systems workers can be the catalyst toward helping many humans become fully balanced and on the path. Be aware, however, that these systems workers must realize the changes brought about by my work (*The End Times,* Chapter Two). With the change in magnetics and enlightenment

opportunity, many of the symptoms of individuals will change, and most of the processes will be able to be accelerated. Those systems workers who ignore this will find their work slowly voided and ineffective... .

(4) The final way to bring about total karmic clearing is through the neutral implant; this was the basic information contained in the first series of translations. This is your new power, and it really is a powerful tool, and very helpful toward the transmutation of negative to positive on your planet.

Now... there is something none of you are experiencing, and I stand amused by it: I have alluded to the fact that we are all part of the whole, and that the number of the whole never changes. There are no new entities. The dynamics of the Universe exist with the numbers that have always been. This is hidden information from you and due to your imprint, you still have difficulty with something that "always was." But it is so. The struggle that you are part of is very old, and is dynamic only to the degree that the **players keep changing faces**. Thus your duality.

What I am trying to say is that while you continue to worship and honor the ancients for their wisdom, and you try to regain the lost information and reveal past hidden secrets, you are your own search. **You are the ancients!** You are the ones who used, and hid, the secrets. You are the ones who left messages and writings for yourselves. Surely there must be some twinge of feeling when you stand over a grave that is your own, or read some ancient writings that you actually wrote. I am amused in love, for your imprints are working so well that you don't recognize yourselves in your own Earth history.

Finally let me speak of death. It is true that each human is biologically unique. That is, you will never have another exactly like your expression after you are gone. This is the main reason you mourn the passing of a loved one. Those who have no concept of the duality, and do not understand the workings of your entities in lesson, have great burdens with the passing of a loved one. For them there is no purpose, and no hope and no peace. Those of you with balance and enlightenment, who fully understand what has happened at death, should still appropriately have ceremony, but it should be in the form of a celebration of the individual's life that has just finished, instead of a morbid empty remembrance without hope or purpose. It is a basic part of your imprint to intuitively realize that "life" goes on after death. When you look at all your Earth-based religions, almost all of them provide this belief. Primitive tribes left to themselves for hundreds of years, that finally emerge in your modern times, carry similar beliefs even though no other individuals have told them anything about religion. It is intuitive, and exists at the cellular level... to realize this fact. This veiled truth is given to you so that you can have peace at the time of human death. Those who stubbornly resist this belief are those who have analyzed their intuition away – these are the ones who stand naked and vulnerable to negativity, for your intuition is your shield against the dark.

When you are able to honor your intuition, and also feel the love we have for you, then you can correctly say good-bye to one who has passed over. When you as workers come together to memorialize a friend, start having the courage to restructure your cultural ceremony and protocol. The "new age" funeral should be something so special and different that all will take note. (1) No physical body or body remains should be present. The carcass no longer has any significance at this point, and is not sacred in any way. Do not burden the Earth with it either. (2) Hold a celebration with all the elements you would normally have at a blessed event. (3) Hold an appropriate meditation prior to, and after the cere-mony, with balanced ones to honor the passed one. Use this time to pray for the planet, for that is the sole purpose of the lesson of the one who has just passed through lesson. Don't be concerned about the emotion you feel. It is all appropriate, and does not indicate weakness of spirit. On the contrary it shows love of the spirit, and honor for the process. (4) Do not encourage a sense of finality, and do not allow any verbalization of negativity. Do not dwell on the past. (5) Show humor in the ceremony, if you are capable.

Some death will be easier than others, but remember that all death is appropriate, even though it may not seem so at the time. If you find yourself in the middle of a situation that seems to be your ultimate horror, where unexpected, seemingly senseless death occurs, then dear one, your awareness of the situation should be doubly heightened, for there is a powerful message there in lesson for you. This is the sign that you are being dealt with at the highest level. This is also a time when many do not "see" the window in this light and "shut down" at a time when they should be moving quickly. Granted, when you are wounded in the heart, and you are still grasping at your chest in hurt and sorrow, it is difficult to do anything but weep. Even still, the Universe has granted you the courage and the strength to rise spiritually at this time, and there is no greater rise than during times such as these. Know this: when something like this occurs for you, or for those around you, then there is purpose and reason at foot. No death is inappropriate. You are all loved without measure, and are all together in a group for reason. To make things even more bizarre for you is the fact that **you helped to plan it all before you got here**. Therefore, consider the situation in total love, and have peace with the event. Your discomfort and loneliness for the one who passed is appropriate and will diminish with time; but the entity lives on, and may even give you signs of this in the weeks and months after the death. **The love you feel for a past one is shared and returned by the past one even after death**. There is nothing wrong with soaking in the love from one who has departed, as long as you do not long for the past. This can be very peaceful and comforting.

This is the hope. This is the reality of love, for the whole never changes, and we continue on and on in love and honor for each other, going through lesson after lesson with singular purpose... coming together planning for the next incarnation, and celebrating the last.

Kryon

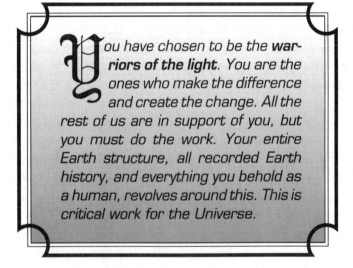

You have chosen to be the **warriors of the light**. You are the ones who make the difference and create the change. All the rest of us are in support of you, but you must do the work. Your entire Earth structure, all recorded Earth history, and everything you behold as a human, revolves around this. This is critical work for the Universe.

Chapter Six

Questions about
Past Lives

Questions about Past Lives

Chapter Six

Question: You have mentioned group karma, and said you would tell more about it later. How does it work?

Answer: This is at the heart of most karmic lessons. It is also one of the most complex of the universal mechanics. It is fully understood and implemented by yourselves, but it is unfortunately difficult to explain to you while in lesson, due to its complexity and your inability to fully comprehend it.

Perhaps some of you have intuitive feelings that many around you have been with you before during past lives... that your mother today was your son before, and your sister before that. This is not illogical or poor thinking. The truth is that it is more apt to be a fact than not. When you consider that you must work through karma with those who set it up in the first place, then you must also realize that you worked together to set it up, and you must also work together to clear it. This requires group entity effort, and therefore group karma. In past incarnations, perhaps you had a father who beat you... or you had those who were dishonest with you... or you made decisions that resulted in the death or suffering of certain individuals. In just these three examples you created complex group karmic ties. These individuals and groups return with you at different times, in different form, to play out their relationship to your karmic imprint.

For instance, your past experience with your father might cause you to feel abandoned today. This feeling is prevalent in your life seemingly for no reason, until you are able to shower love on your daughter... who might just be your returned father. Sometimes the group member is just a catalyst, and does not return with you. They only plant the seed for you to work through, and play no part in the clearing. Other times, and most often, they play an active part in the clearing, but not always as in the father example – (of being the object of the clearing). The idea that karma is always role reversal from lifetime to lifetime is not accurate. Killers don't come back to be killed, and wrongdoers don't come back to be wronged. Just the opposite is most likely; that is, you often get another chance to be wronged by the same group, and to work through it and come out enlightened. Can you see how working through it could also affect them? This is also their part of the clearing, or opportunity for clearing. All this has to do with intuition, taking power where it is available, and eventual full enlightenment of self. If you made bad decisions that hurt people, you may have the same opportunity again. But this time you get a chance to let intuition and conscience rule, rather than ego or emotion.

In the case of those who did you wrong... perhaps they have come back in similar life positions as an opportunity for you to react differently to them, thereby "clearing" the fear connected with the past events. Many times group members will appear in your life only for a short time just to "trigger" the clearing, thereby helping their own karmic clearing as well.

There is also a great deal of singular event-driven karma. An example of this would be a violent death by falling or drowning. The next expression may find you with great fear of falling or being drowned, even though you can see no reason why this should be so. These are also fears to be worked through, and they deal greatly with intuitive trust of the workings of the Universe in your life, and not with others around you. These are what I have described as the "phantoms" of your expression. These are fears that are baseless, and exist only for the process of being cleared.

The reason why all of this is so complex is that there are tremendous interactive attributes between individuals and groups. Obviously the groups overlap, and if you have found yourself traveling from place to place all your life, you might wonder how the groups can relate to you... but they still do. Everywhere you go there is someone who is in place there to help you in some way, and vice versa. In addition to this complexity, there is the added dimension of Earth time. Some entities come in to spend their lives with you. Some come in to be in your life only for a short time and then death occurs. Some come in just for the sole purpose of dying! In all cases, there are lessons surrounding each coming and going, and as mentioned, there are especially powerful lessons of opportunity around dramatic events such as death, trauma, war, and natural disaster. This time factor demands that entities wait to reincarnate, sometimes for much of a lifetime so that they can be very young while you are older. After you pass, there is another group for them to relate to. Can you see the complexity? It is much like a three-dimensional chess game with thousands of pieces, each with a different move assignment. One interacts with many, and many interact with one.

This is why when you lose loved ones or friends, you have no concept if they are going to return quickly or actually wait until most of the group is with them. In addition to all this, you have the physical placement on the Earth to consider. All of you at one time or another have been part of the great civilizations of the planet. Many times it has been with the same group, but not always. As a rule, the groups tend to stay together to facilitate lesson, but you will still meet people on the other side of the Earth whom you feel you know, who might have been "stand-ins" for another entity who moved on or graduated. A stand-in is one who incarnates in place of a group member who is finished, to facilitate the same karma that the one who couldn't return was scheduled to do. The stand-in is a very different kind of individual, and often will appear unbalanced to society. This is a human playing out karma that is not his, for the benefit of those around him who need it.

Regarding the phenomenon you call "walk ins," there are two scenarios: (1) When appropriate, there are those who "take over" during an incarnation, because an existing human is finished with karma and can leave. But to the Universe it is more valuable for timing reasons to "swap souls" within the same body to allow another to come in without biological birth. This is most common after an extended coma, or life changing dream of some kind. (2) It is also common for the same entity to reincarnate within the same human during the same lifetime! This often follows a near death experience, or trauma of some kind where human death was seemingly averted, and the individual seems to be changed forever due to the experience. Both of these are methods used by the Universe to accelerate group karmic timing.

One obvious question you might have is about the physical numbers of humans. I have told you that the whole never changes, but there are far more now than before, so where did they come from? The answer here is even more complex. They were in lesson elsewhere, and probably in a star group. Remember, your service to the Universe is that of one who is a warrior of light. You constantly move into and out of lesson... and I didn't specify that it was always the Earth. When you graduate here, you may move on to be in lesson somewhere else.

In conclusion to your question, dear one, be aware that those around you who are playing an active part in your life are most likely old souls who have been with you many times. Does this give you a different perspective on them?

Question: I know you have already partially answered the question about the masses who are dying now on the planet, but can you elaborate? I am still having trouble with this.

Answer: You will always have a reaction to death, even appropriate death, for it represents Earth pain and suffering, and biological hardship. Never feel that you will be without this empathy, for it is part of your balance. It is appropriate and correct that you should feel sorrow for these souls in hardship, and it is honored that you wish to prevent their plight.

There is nothing whatsoever you can do to prevent large groups of humans from perishing at this time. It has already begun, and will continue for years. There is great unreported death happening now, even as you read this, and it is part of the overall scenario for the planet. In the previous series I spoke of this more than once. I told you then that up to one percent of the entire globe was involved over a period of time. This represents entire karmic groups, groups that have no hope whatsoever of receiving enlightenment or proceeding on the path. The irony here is that in the old energy these groups could remain; now the new energy demands that they leave. There is no forward motion for them, and no learning. It is appropriate, and their souls are anxious to move on.

These are groups who knew this might happen when they came in, and they gave great purpose to that end. These special groups that you are feeling anxious for are going to immediately return as gifted humans of the indigo color aura. This termination is going to help the planet immensely, and is actually part of your new opportunity, and the transmutation process as previously discussed. I realize and understand the paradox in all of this for you, for you are creatures of love, born in the spirit, and you are meant to follow humanitarian purposes. Do what you can for these, but do not despair over their plight, for it has honor of purpose, especially for the children. Observe everything in universal wisdom. Weep if it serves you, but eventually come to mature understanding of the way of things in the larger overall picture.

Question: Is there anything new that you can tell us about past-life mechanics that may help us now or in the future?

Answer: I will give insight for those who deal with past-life clearing. There is a human attribute that also is a soul attribute. Some of you previously have determined that a human has a time cycle while on Earth that is either fast or slow or somewhere in between. You measure it in years. You use this to help explain why a person takes a very long time to make changes, or does so quickly. This is not the variable you might expect. Although you are mostly correct in the method of determining the cycle for an individual, what you do not know is that the time cycle will also be the same for that soul. It will be the same for that soul each time it comes into expression. It was the same in the last expression, and it will be the same in the next. This is a soul attribute and relates to universal pattern of vibration as well as your time cycle on Earth. It is one of the several attributes that are carried into expression that belong to the soul, and are permanent. This attribute is not biological, but is universal in its origin. I cannot explain this pattern variable that belongs to entities such as myself, and yourself, for it deals with terminology and concepts that are not comprehensible for you in lesson.

The new information is that there is also a cyclical lifetime pattern that matches the time cycle. If you know a person is a 3 time cycle, then you should also look for significant lifetimes of karmic importance in groups of three as measured backward from the current one. Not every lifetime is one of tremendous karmic importance. In fact, most are not. That is why many humans live uneventful lives without apparent upheaval, distress, learning, clearing, or enlightenment. Many lifetimes are lived as rest periods between the ones that are meaningful. Remember that time is not important to us. It is only an Earth concept, and therefore what seems like a very long and arduous process to you is all in the "now" for us. Your soul needs periods of light karmic involvement between the heavy ones just as you need balance in Earthly things for health.

What this means to you as a worker is that you can better target the meaningful lifetimes for examination. If you know the person's time cycle, look for the same cycle for significant lifetimes, the ones that are causing the fear and trouble now. This is also a secret to the kind of karmic lessons that are involved. Those with long time cycles (such as a 9) would tend to have heavier karmic attributes fall on every ninth lifetime, and they are more prone to need help with clearing them. A person with a 2 time cycle will have more attributes spread over every second lifetime, and will be more able to clear them with everyday living. Look for tragedy and physical specter with the longer time cycles, and more human interrelated karma with the faster cycles. These are generalities, and as with all karma, there are exceptions based on the groups... but basically this information will serve you.

Question: You mean that some of us regularly take on heavier karma than the others? This somehow doesn't seem fair.

Answer: Remember when I spoke of your cultural assumptions getting in the way of clear logical thinking? This is a prime case. Who informed you that every soul gets a turn at every karmic lesson? Hardly! Just as there is specialization in service, there are also attributes within your service group. You are all very, very different on this side of the veil than you are in human form. Perhaps you thought that all entities on my side were white-robed figures with blank faces?

Our diversity would startle you. Just as I have described our different colors to you in the past, we each also have names, shapes, services, and things that we are very good at. You know these things, but they are hidden from you. Don't you understand that your biology is patterned after a bigger picture? Do you think you would be provided such a variety of personality types on Earth just to return to some mundane generic sameness on this side of the veil? There is great humor over this visualization!

I love you dearly, and wish to inform you more on the subject of karma and how it relates to lifetimes. Know these things: your soul entity is a specialist in lesson. At the soul level some are equipped for fewer heavy lessons, and some are equipped for a myriad of smaller ones, just like humans are equipped with different attributes. Generally it works like this: there are three basic groups for karmic consideration – the 1 to 3 group, the 4 to 6 group, and the 7 to 9 group. There is no cycle higher than the nine. If you find a human who does not fit into a repeating cycle, then you could be dealing with a special few souls who have multiple attributes, and can vary the cycles if desired.

Those with cycles from 1 to 3 are sent in with an appropriate karmic imprint to allow for fast turnaround of many small but potent lessons. These more frequent lessons deal with interrelations with others in lesson. You know these, dear ones, for they are all around you. These are the ones who need to clear the attributes of what has happened with those who have abused them, and those they have abused. They have serious on-going current lifetime problems with parents or children, or other relatives or friends. They seem to be perpetual victims, or feel they need to strike out and get even, or constantly defend themselves. This is the kind of karma in the 1 to 3 group. As you might expect, the 1 gets a slightly different dose that the 3. Those in this group who are able to clear the karmic imprint will most likely be involved in helping others on a spiritual basis. All of these need to learn the important lesson of tolerance, a difficult one for all humans.

The 4 to 6 group is more evenly spread in all types of karma. These not only get to have some of the human situations to work through, like the 1-3 group, but they also get to have some heavier events to consider with it. These are the ones who must also work through lessons that deal with more violence, usually human against human. Perhaps they burned someone to death in the name of God, or worse yet, learned to use negativity for control of others. They are the ones who often meet terrible death at the hands of other humans. There are many leaders here, and many humanitarians. Their main lesson is one of forgiveness... of others and of themselves. There are more of these than of the others.

The 7 to 9 group get the heavy Earth karma. They also figure highly in leadership positions of all kinds, but often die violently, due to accidents such as falling, burning, or drowning. Their lessons are mostly to overcome the big fear they carry over from these past events. The fear is so great it often makes them appear unbalanced in their current lifetime. These are the ones most likely to become mentally sick – or totally balanced. The reason for this is that they carry such heavy attributes that action of some kind is usually demanded to exist even at the most basic level of normalcy. The reason they are often leaders is that they seek power as a method to gain control over their fear.

I would not be Kryon if I did not remind you of the numerology here. The group totals are 4-1-7, and that totals 3, the number of manifestation and action.

All groups feature some fear, for it is a human staple of karma. I have spoken often of the phantom fears of lesson, and by that I mean the seed fears that you all carry, such as being discounted or abandoned, being alone, and failing or falling short of what is expected. These fears are common to all.

Remember the immediate message of my work here: the new power of your neutral implant can void almost all of these karmic workings. If you have not received this new information, then seek it out! It is the good news of the new window of opportunity for the planet, and is for all humanity. It is your earned gift!

Question: Does this correlate with the time cycle computations that modern workers are doing now? What computation basis are you referring to?

Answer: An entity time cycle is absolute information, and not open to groups of computational variance. What does vary, however, are the layers of meanings associated with the numbers that belong to the formula.

The main formula you are using now, by way of the methods of Nepal, are simply derivatives of the method given to those of the civilization of the Indus Valley over 4,000 years ago. This group remained for only 600 years, but embraced a universal faith that prevailed, and eventually spread over a very wide area. Like many other benign civilizations, they left themselves open to being conquered by others of lesser wisdom, and were decimated. Although their doctrine lay dormant for many years, it had a mutated rebirth in some other areas including Nepal, and carried with it the seeds of the system you now use. Try working backwards from your modern computations to discover the seed base. This will give you better insight into interpretation, but won't necessarily demand change of your current process. When I say work backwards, I mean for you to take a hard look at the assumptions within the formula. This examination will eventually reveal some hidden information about how the process was originally used, and new ways to apply and interpret it.

If you wish to know more about the enlightenment of the Indus Valley group, then find out how they laid out their cities. This quest will give you a glimpse into the cosmic humor I often speak of... for it relates to the Kryon work.

Kryon

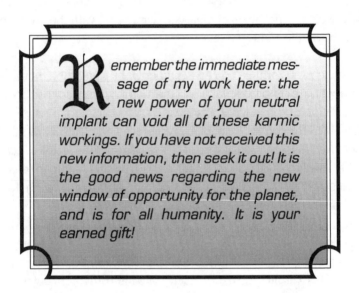

Remember the immediate message of my work here: the new power of your neutral implant can void all of these karmic workings. If you have not received this new information, then seek it out! It is the good news regarding the new window of opportunity for the planet, and is for all humanity. It is your earned gift!

Chapter Seven

Lemuria
and
Atlantis

Lemuria & Atlantis
Chapter Seven

There has been much good information given to you about Lemuria and Atlantis, but the information I have may give it a different perspective. I previously told you that I had been here doing my work three other times. It is now time to reveal the workings of this. The first time I was here was to set up the magnetic grid system under the authorization of the group that has control of such things. It was a wonderful time, filled with great science and spectacular workings. Earth was old enough, and stable, and ready for the system.

I had great help, and there were some of you who assisted in a large way to make the initial system work. It was at this time that the cave of creation was set up, and a list made of all the entities who would share the planet, both above and below. This was a truly great planning effort, and everything was done in love and expectation. It is so with any planetary setup, but your planet was special in that it was to be the "only planet of free choice." None had been this way.

Your imprint and implants are designed to keep your aware-ness cloudy and simple, and are designed to make you actively search for truth. This same situation makes you think of God and the Universe as a perfect place. You believe that everything is pre-planned, and you have marked tendencies toward a theory of predestination because of this. Nothing of the kind is so. There is a great deal of interaction that is only known as it happens. I have spoken about the mechanics of Earth lesson, and about how you incarnate to learn. Many of you learn; some of you do not. The effort is the work, and the realization is the fruit, but no entity knows the outcome.

Because you set up the lessons, there is a plan at work when it comes to whom you are with... what happens while you are here... who you are... where you live... and who experiences Earth death... and when. There is also control to some degree over large Earth events, since we (Universe) understand how the planet works internally and externally. How you fare while you are here is totally up to you, and is unknown by anyone.

There is also a great deal of "working around" what we (Universe) know will naturally happen regarding Earth in general, but that we do not cause to happen. So you see, there is much planning and work that has gone into preparing the classroom for your lessons, but make no mistake: **we don't control** your lessons. We do, however, control the classroom. Remember that I said how honored you were for your work of the last half century? This was not foretold, and it has created great excitement. My return was expected, but it was for an entirely different adjustment. I cannot contain my honor, celebration and love when I realize I have returned here to align for power instead of termination. Endless activity is happening all around you that has to do with these changes. Entities from all over the Universe are arriving to serve you. Whereas you were sinking into the dark, you have surfaced to strike out with new power in the light. You have no idea what this means to the universal plan. You have no idea how honored you will be when you finally leave lesson on Earth. There is no energy potent enough I can send you that can be translated properly on this issue.

When we finished setting the grids, and the first humans received their soul imprints, it was a marvelous thing. It took place much further back than any of you realize, and you have no evidence of this first civilization anywhere. Someday, when the Earth churns it up and delivers the evidence to the surface, you as incarnate humans will be long gone.

Even though Earth had evolved humanoid biology early on, it needed help with your type later, from other human biological types of high-lesson vibration from another planet. This is not important for you to understand at this time, other than to say that your current **human** biology is not entirely Earth-born, and that these dear ones who shared their seed have watched you for eons with love and concern. Their seed was necessary for your DNA to respond to Universal stimulus, and to make the differentiation in your consciousness between beasts and humans. This is the "missing link" you will not find until it finally shows itself.

After your civilization was set up, it was expected that I would return for an adjustment, for just as you currently have no pre-knowledge of how you will do in lesson, we had no pre-knowledge of how your new biology would fare in the created energy of the grid system as originally set up. When I was summoned again, it was to terminate life and readjust. This may sound harsh to you, but it was all appropriate and expected. What exactly happened (you might ask)?

The grid system at that time gave far too much tolerance for enlightenment than we had anticipated. The system you have now is very well balanced for your soul lesson, and has been that way for thousands of years. It took two major adjustments to get it correct, and the first one dealt with the termination of the civilization of Lemuria and Atlantis. Although people were very far apart on Earth, and were of different ages, most of the humans had something in common: they were very aware of enlightened science. Some (*The Atlantians*) were close to a very high vibra-tion communication with their soul entities, but without knowl-edge of what it all meant. This did not serve lesson at all, and very little was being **learned**. Instead, it was all being **given** (*absorbed naturally through a very weak veil*). The veil was not in place anywhere near the degree it had to be, and most of the humans had automatic answers to the tests instead of having to learn them and implement them. We allowed this to remain a very long time in hopes of self-correction, so as not to create the additional karma that would be later associated with the termination; but it did not happen in this manner. This first grid alignment caused an odd combination of enlightenment and imbalance that gave a civilization of humans with weak duality in some areas, and strong in others. It allowed for slavery next to high spiritual science, and a feeling of power without realization of its source. In addition, through science the elite humans of the time achieved a much longer life span, and this was not productive or appropriate for what the planet was designed for. The elite lived long lives, equal to 5 or 6 generations of their slaves, which slowly became unlike humans at all. The elite did not share the science. Accompanying my realignment was the total destruction of the land masses associated with the civilization, and an allowance for a short Earth cyclical ice period and accompanying crust action to plow under any remaining remnants of the event. We then allowed as long a cycle to lapse as there had been civilization, in order to balance the planet again.

I remained the entire time, and again we had seeds from the others to create your appropriate biology. Then toward the end of your last short ice cycle, we again launched another adjusted magnetic alignment that was much more biased toward less initial enlightenment and self-realization. In other words, the duality (the veil) was strengthened. In the years that followed I was again summoned for service to the planet (*my third visit*), since a smaller correction was needed to adjust for a slightly higher vibration. This time there was an abundance of karma being created, but very little karma was being worked through. The duality was slightly overbalanced on the strong side (*no awareness of the veil at all*). This created a totally unenlightened population, and again Earth had no chance to be raised in vibration. Only a very few were aware of any spirituality at all. The goal was not being served. I was then brought back to make the final alignment adjustment. This last alignment was not that long ago, and you have it on record as your world flood. Human biology was preserved and perpetuated through this time, and although much surface life was terminated, the flood did not cover all the land as you have been led to believe. This last alignment is what you have grown up in, and it has remained until now, where it is again being changed and realigned to allow you to take your power and move into the final stages of planetary graduation! Now you know the chronology of the Kryon group, and the basic reasons for my four visits to you.

Dear ones, if all of this sounds fantastic, it is not important for you to understand it. It is simple history and fact. The only thing that **is** important is for you to understand the significance of why I am here **now**. The status of the Earth at this moment carries with it vast importance to the universal working of things. This love source that I speak of time and time again represents the heart of all things. Nothing can ever separate us from this source. All that has been before, and will be in the future, is done to enhance and increase this love energy. Now as never before you have the power while on Earth to collectively make a difference to the planet, to others, and to yourselves. While you do it, the love will pour into you and your minds will be rewarded with the greatest gift humans have ever been able to receive from us... that is, the peace of the singular love source, the peace of God, and the tolerance and wisdom of eons of entity experience!

This gift is a powerful one, for it will allow you to continue to work and live within the arrangement you are used to, but with increased power and peace. These are your times, bought and paid for with thousands of years of incarnations and work by yourselves. Claim this time. You are empowered to do so.

I love you dearly.   *Kryon*

*See pages 107, 153, 160, 275, and Appendix A for information about the Atlantis "Temple of Rejuvenation."

Chapter Eight

Questions about
our
Past

Questions About Our Past
Chapter Eight

Question: You spoke of karma that would be created by the Lemurian and Atlantian termination. What kind of karma do we carry now in this lifetime because of it?

Answer: All of you who were part of those ancient times (and there were a great many of you) carry the seed fear of **termination due to enlightenment**. Remember that karma is a lesson. Strong Earth karma is often manifested through feelings that we cannot understand at the moment, such as fear of water, heights, small spaces, fire, etc. These are holdovers from trauma of past life experiences, and they serve us (*the Universe*) when you realize what is causing them, and conquer the fear. This is the transmutation process that raises the level of the planet's vibration.

All karma is hidden until exposed, and all karma is dealt with while in lesson as part of the duality while on Earth. The Termination of Lemuria and Atlantis left a very strong cause-and-effect relationship between enlightenment and death. This "seed fear" is only now being worked through, since you are only now coming into the kind of power that would be a familiar feeling to you... and many of you are reacting to it with fear. Let me give you an example of how you workers might be feeling: perhaps you have been doing the work for many years, but as of this year you are becoming lethargic. Small doses of depression are working themselves into periods between your sessions. You suddenly lack desire or direction, and there is an unspoken heaviness that accompanies situations that have the most potential for success. You find yourselves actually alarmed at the numbers of individuals who are beginning to realize the duality. This is a strange, familiar feeling, and you are waiting for the axe to fall, or as some humans say, "for the other shoe to drop." You proceed with full knowledge that your actions are appropriate, but deep within yourselves you are uncomfortable. This is classic fear karma, and represents the seed fear of the Lemurian and Atlantian termination.

My advice to you is as it has been all along: get in touch with your guides for immediate peace over this situation. Call for the neutral implant, or at least face the fear and work through it. You can have a wonderful healing experience over this fear, and release it completely, if you will face it down and ask your guides in total love to give you the implant to release it. As stated in earlier writings, many of you are receiving new guides at this time, whose sole purpose is to give you peace over this newly realized seed fear. These new guides are very specialized, for they represent a master service that deals with the karmic lessons of self-realization and power. If you could see the activity around the Earth, it would amaze you.

Question: With all of this universal activity, why can't our scientists see something happening? Is it all too far beyond our senses?

Answer: I will never give you information that will expose the duality, or raise questions for the Earth scientists to ponder that would risk the new level of learning that you are in. However, I can tell you that master entities leave a residue when arriving. Look for short, highly intense, unexplainable gamma ray activity.*

Question: You spoke about our cyclical ice periods. I suppose we had a number of these in history. What causes them?

Answer: Before I answer this, you must put into perspective the time line of lesson. Your Earth was old and mature when your civilization was planted. All of your work and all of your civilizations have taken place within the last 250,000 Earth years, and yet the Earth is far older than this. In all my time coming and going, I have only observed one ice cycle; but there have been many.

*see page 228

Your ice cycles are caused by Earth shifting its orbit around the sun to a new ellipse, much like the orbit of the small outer planet you call Pluto. I will not give you the actual cause of the orbit shift, but suffice to say that it is cyclical, and will happen again. Please do not concern yourself with it, however, since the event is very, very far away. There was method in the timing we chose to set the grids when we did.

Question: You spoke of the cave of creation. What is it? ... and where is it?

Answer: This has to do with "energy accounting," to use a human term. This is a very sacred place where the real entity names for all of you are kept while you are in lesson. This is necessary for the duality and is a very real, physical place on Earth. It is carefully guarded, and if humans were to somehow stumble on it, they would be terminated in a similar fashion to the human who touched the Ark of the Covenant. The famous ancient Ark had a very similar attribute, and contained a similar energy. It was a traveling temple that held the balance of the entities' power of the tribes it traveled with. Humans are now able to carry the **entire** entity power and enlightenment, and all they have to do is discover it. But back then they were not able to carry it, and the balance of it was stored in the temples and on the grids. The ancient stories you hear of the magic and power within the temples had great truth to them. Only the priests could enter for these reasons, and although these priests were really no more enlightened than the others, they were protected by their master guides (whose service was to do just that). The intensity was too great for most to endure. This situation has long since changed, and there is less entity power storage going on than in any time in history.

The cave is under a tropical part of the Earth, but very, very deep and unreachable. There are no passageways or tunnels to it, and there are no human access attributes. It may be interesting for you to know that you (*my partner*) have been taken there three times since your birth in this lesson. It is a favorite place for your guides to take humans when they are ready. From this standpoint it is accessible to most humans at an astral level, but only during times when they are receiving implants or guide changes... or coming or going. Again, it has to do with power and entity accounting. It is the first place you see when you die, and the first place you see when you are conceived. It glows a very bright white and is closely attended by those also in white. The human close-to-death experiences are related to this cave, and deal almost exclusively with the trip to it, and experiencing the feelings surrounding it. The universal names and attributes of all in Earth lesson are stored here.

I tell you these things freely, with the absolute knowledge that this cave will not be found. It has been placed for your safety. You may eventually be able to measure its existence with your scientific instruments, but you can never reach it.

Question: When you say that you were "summoned" here, it would indicate that you answer to a higher power. Who sent for you, and where are you from?

Answer: There is no higher "power" than the singular source, and you have that within yourselves. I respond to requests by the group that oversees planets in lesson. I am a technician in service for this group, whose name can be translated loosely as the "Brothers of Light." Names such as these, as I have told you earlier, are very subject to interpretation, since they are not absolute names in any language on Earth. It would be like naming a color, and expecting it to remain that exact name throughout all history in all cultures and languages, no matter who interpreted its hues.

There is no authority structure. We all carry the same authority and wisdom. This is not an Earth cultural concept, and so until you are out of lesson, I cannot expect that you would know of this, or understand it. It is much like your biological body, however. You are not aware of a boss telling your parts what to do, but you are aware of a central unit that provides for the coordination of your biological balance. None of your parts have to agree, and none of your parts rebel. Everything works in unison toward the goal of life sustenance, and all the parts respect and work with the others. Your consciousness is a whole sum of your parts, and you would find it silly at the thought of your heart not sending blood to your feet when they needed it, or having your liver tell your brain it was going to form a body of its own.

There is no human-type interaction that describes the interaction of the entities of the Universe. All the political and emotional human interaction was created for your lesson, and is typically your own.

I am from the center. I am from the "core," or central creative force, where the love source emanates. I belong to no specific part of the Universe, and I am not to be identified with any specific group other than that of service to you.

Question: You have spoken before about your "support group." Are these the guides, or do you have an actual group that works with you on grid alignment? Where are they?

Answer: This is one of the most humorous questions you (*my partner*) have ever asked! In total love I salute you for your duality! You do not remember your own command, and you do not know of your service with me. Such is the wonder of your sacrifice of lesson, and we love you for this.

My support group will remain veiled from all of you, but I can tell you that it is a large contingent of entities who are working with me to accomplish the gradual realignment of your magnetics. In addition, it is the work of this group to pass information to the arriving entities from all over the Universe as to the attributes of your new energy at this time. My support group is located in the orbit of Jupiter around the sun.

Question: Dare I ask the question of who are the ones who helped us with the seed biology from elsewhere in the Universe?

Answer: This is not a secret, and has been known for some time. They are your close neighbors from the group of stars you call the "Seven Sisters." These are your actual biological ancestors, and are very much part of your family. This will remain controversial knowledge until the end. The reason is that their duality is much weaker than yours, and their planet is in graduate lesson, with a great deal of enlightenment... the attributes we believe your planet is heading for.

What this means is that they have been in graduate status for more than 250,000 of your Earth years. They are in lesson, one that deals with things other than karma, but still requires human-like biology. There is birth and death, just like your planet, but they have gone through the tests. They exist almost solely to provide seed help, and at times to provide technical and biological intervention, a process that I will not explain at this time.

They visit often, but like me, there is restraint regarding revealing too much in areas you have not yet ventured... so that you will do it yourselves in your own linear time, and reap the rewards accordingly.

Kryon

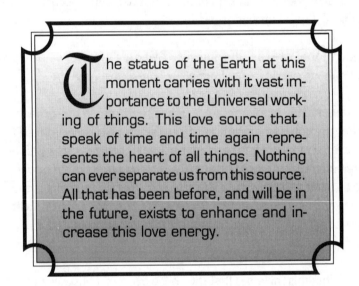

The status of the Earth at this moment carries with it vast importance to the Universal working of things. This love source that I speak of time and time again represents the heart of all things. Nothing can ever separate us from this source. All that has been before, and will be in the future, exists to enhance and increase this love energy.

Chapter Nine

Self-Discovery

Self-Discovery
Chapter Nine

I f all this book concerned itself with was self-discovery, then it would be complete, for this is the most important subject for each of you. It does not deal with finding the "best" in you, or finding "self-worth," or any of the intellectual items that your medical helpers deal with. This subject deals with finding the bridge between the human "you" and the universal "you" as described earlier in the duality discussion. Finding this bridge will change your whole life, including how you feel about yourself, others, and the Earth. It will also give a far wiser perspective on what you might do with the rest of your life in order to raise the vibration of the planet. In short, it is everything for you. It is the prime directive at this time, and is a fast "work-through" for your remaining karma.

Many of you spend a great deal of time trying to understand the workings of things, and the history and meaning of things. Some of you spend huge amounts of energy and riches in the endeavor to solve unexplained phenomena, or the mystical meanings of ob-  jects and structures left for you to ponder. This is your human intellectual approach to apparent self-discovery, under the pretense that if you know about these things, then you will know about yourself. It also represents that part of you that wants verification on a logical human basis of things you do not understand, so that you can better relate to the whole picture. Although these methods served you well in the past energies, they are of limited value in the new energy. You still don't understand how your brain works... but you can't very well deny its viability just because you can't explain it; and of course the irony is that you have to use it to question it.

Now comes a time for you to grasp the essence and emotion of who you are and really see as much of the "piece of God" that is you which you are allowed to see in lesson. As previously mentioned, this is easier now and is offered to all who are ready, instead of just a selected few. Because of this, the subject of your self-discovery is dripping with potency, excitement and fulfilled dreams. This is your "take-charge" action that is felt but not analyzed, and it is the new gift that is standing before you, waiting for you to acknowledge. However it requires courage to move through your fear of it.

It does not replace the intellectual pursuit, but it enhances it greatly. It has only been in the past few years that some of your Earth scientists have followed an entirely different method in their thinking, and it would serve you to follow suit regarding your own self-discovery. In the past the hypothesis of an apparent scientific mystery had to be solved before scientists could further hypothesize about something within the mystery, or next to the mystery. This forced everyone to stop thinking until the first mystery was solved. Your forward-thinking scientists have realized that this kind of human compartmentalization of logic is flawed for certain types of examination (such as that of small particle behavior). Now when they reach a point of apparent dichotomous results based on careful experimentation... they simply move past it without a reasonable explanation, but knowing that one exists, and that perhaps it will show itself if they continue to look further into the puzzle, even though they don't know what they are looking for. They base their further experimentation not on the workings of known mechanics, but on the probability of past observed behavior, and expected future behavior, even though it is not understood. This is **trust**.

It is with this attitude, therefore, that I address and challenge even the most intellectual of you. If you will endeavor to go through the exercise of "feeling" who you are, and verbally asking your guides to assist you in the process, you will emerge on the other side with tremendous wisdom of how to proceed with the intellectual side of it as well. I would never ask any of you to sacrifice that logical part of you that wishes to know about truth. What I will ask you to do is to learn how to fly the vehicle, and feel what it's like to soar to unimaginable heights. Then you can land, open the engine, and try to find out how it all worked.

What follows is a metaphor in the form of a parable. It contains many facets regarding your human condition in regard to life itself, and especially about self-discovery. It also paints a picture, for those of you who are insightful, of how the Universe works and responds to you. If you are puzzled by any of this, then ask your guides for its meaning. What follows is given in love.

The Room of Lesson

There once was a human whom we will call Wo. Wo's gender is not important to this story; but since you do not have an adequate word for a neutral gendered person, we call the human Wo... to encompass a man called Wo, or a Wo-man. For translation only, however, we will say Wo is a him.

As all humans in his culture Wo lived in a house, but Wo was really only concerned with the room that he lived in, since it was uniquely his own. His room was beautiful and he was charged with keeping it that way... which he did.

Wo lived a good life; he was in a culture where he never wanted for food, for it was plentiful. He also never was cold, for he always had cover. As Wo grew up he learned many things about himself. He learned the things that made him feel happy, and he would find objects to hang on the wall that he could look at, to make him happy. Wo also learned of the things that made him feel sad, and he learned how to hang these things on the wall when he wished to be sad. Wo also learned the things that made him angry, and he found things to drag out and place on the wall that he could turn to when he chose to be angry.

As with other humans, Wo had many fears. Even though he had the basics in life, he feared other humans and certain situations. He feared the humans and situations that could bring change, for he felt secure and stable with the way things were, and he had worked hard to get them to that state. Wo feared the situations that seemingly had control over his stable room, and he feared the humans who controlled these situations.

He learned about God from the other humans. They told him that being a human was a very small thing, and Wo believed it. After all, he looked around him and saw millions of humans, but only one God. He was told that God was everything and that he was nothing, but that God in his infinite love would answer Wo's prayers if he prayed in earnest and had integrity during his life. So Wo, being a spiritual person, prayed to God that the humans and situations he feared would not create changes, so his room could remain without change... and God answered Wo's request.

Wo feared the past for somehow it reminded him of unpleasant things; so he prayed to God to block these things from his memory... and God answered Wo's request. Wo also feared the future for it contained potential for change, and was dark, uncertain and hidden from him. Wo prayed to God that the future would not bring change to his room... and God answered his request.

Wo never ventured very far into his room for all he really needed as a human was in one corner. When his friends came to visit, this is the corner he showed to them... and he was satisfied with this.

Wo first noticed motion in the other corner when he was about 26. It frightened him severely and he immediately prayed to God for it to go away, for it suggested that he was not alone in his room. This was not an acceptable condition. God answered Wo's request and the motion stopped, and Wo did not fear it anymore.

When he was 34 it returned, and again Wo asked that it be stopped, for he was very afraid. The motion stopped, but not before Wo saw something he had missed completely in the corner... another door! On the door was strange writing, and Wo feared its implications.

Wo asked religious leaders about the strange door and the motion, and they warned him not to go near it, for they said it was the door of death, and he would certainly die if his curiosity became action. They also told him the writing on the door was evil, and that he should never look on it again. Instead they encouraged him to participate in ritual with them, and give of his talent and earnings to the group... and for this they told him he would fare well.

When Wo was 42 the motion again returned. Although Wo wasn't as afraid of it this time, he again asked for it to stop... and it did. God was good to answer so completely and quickly. Wo felt empowered by the results of his prayers.

When Wo was 50, he became ill and died, although he wasn't really aware of it when it happened. He noticed the motion again in the corner, and again prayed for it to stop; but instead it became clearer and came closer. In fear Wo arose from his bed only to discover that his Earth body remained, and he was in spirit form. As the motion came closer, Wo started somehow to recognize it. He was curious instead of frightened, and his spirit body seemed somehow natural.

Wo now saw that the motion was actually two entities who approached. The white figures gleamed as though they had a light from within, as they drew closer. Finally they stood before him, and Wo was astounded by their majesty... but he wasn't afraid.

One of the figures spoke to Wo and said "Come, dear one, it's time to go." The figure's voice was poignant with gentleness and familiarity. Without hesitation Wo went with the two. He was starting to remember how familiar all this was... as he looked behind him and saw his carcass seemingly asleep on the bed. He was filled with a wonderful feeling, and could not explain it. One of the entities took his hand and led him directly toward the door with the strange writing on it. The door opened and all three went through it.

He found himself in a long hallway with doors to rooms on each side. Wo thought to himself, "This is indeed a far larger house than I had imagined!" Wo noticed the first door with more odd writing on it. He spoke to one of the white ones. "What is in this first door on the right?" Without a word the white figure opened the door and motioned for Wo to enter. As Wo entered he was amazed. Stacked from floor to ceiling were riches beyond his wildest dreams! There were gold bars, pearls and diamonds. In one corner alone there were enough rubies and precious stones for an entire kingdom. He looked at his white, glowing companions and said "What is this place?" The larger white one spoke and said, "This is your room of abundance, had you wished to enter it. It belongs to you even now and will remain here for you in the future." Wo was startled by this information.

As they returned to the hallway Wo asked what was in the first room to the left... another door with writing that somehow was starting to make sense. As the white one opened the door he said "This is your room of peace, had you wished to use it." Wo entered the room with his friends, only to be surrounded by a thick white fog. The fog seemed to be alive, for it immediately encased his body, and Wo breathed it in. He was overcome with comfort, and knew he would never be afraid again. He felt peace where there had never been any before. He wanted to stay, but his companions motioned for him to continue, and they again started down the long hallway.

Still another door on the left. "What is this room?" Wo asked. "It is a place where only you can go," said the smaller white figure. Wo entered the room and was immediately filled with a gold light. He knew what this was. This was Wo's self essence, his enlightenment, his knowledge of past and future. This was Wo's storehouse of spirit and love. Wo wept with joy, and stood absorbing truth and understanding for a very long time. His companions did not come in, and were patient.

Finally Wo again stepped into the hallway. He had changed. He looked at his companions and recognized them. "You are the guides," Wo stated matter of factly. "No," said the large one, "we are **your** guides." In perfect love they continued. "We have been here since your birth for only one reason: to love you and help show you the doorway. You were afraid and asked for us to retreat, and we did. We are in service to you in love, and we honor your incarnation of expression." Wo felt no reprimand in their words. He realized that they were not in judgment of him, but in honor of him, and he felt their love.

Wo looked at the doors and was now able to read the writing! As he was led down the hallway there were doors marked HEALING, CONTRACT, and another marked JOY. Wo saw even more than he had wished, for down the line there were doors with names of unborn children... and even one marked WORLD LEADER. Wo began to realize what he had missed. And as if they knew his thoughts, the guides said, "Do not be reproachful with your spirit, for it is inappropriate and does not serve your magnificence." Wo did not fully understand. He looked back down the hallway from where he had first entered and saw the writing on the door, the writing that had originally frightened him. The writing was a name! ... it was **his** name, his real name... and He now fully understood.

Wo knew the routine, for now He remembered everything, and He was no longer Wo. He said good-bye to his guides and thanked them for their faithfulness. He stood for a long time looking at them and loving them. Then He turned to walk toward the light at the end of the hallway. He had been here before. He knew what was waiting for him on his brief three-day trip to the cave of creation to retrieve his essence... and then on to the hall of honor and celebration, where those who loved him dearly were waiting for him, including those whom He had loved and lost while on Earth.

He knew where he had been, and where he was going. Wo was going home.

Kryon

• For an analysis of this parable, please see Appendix B

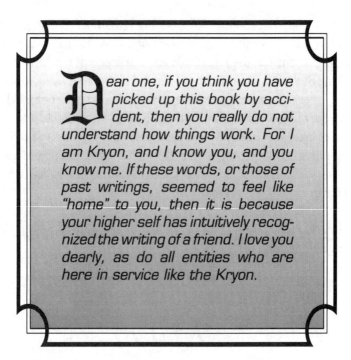

Dear one, if you think you have picked up this book by accident, then you really do not understand how things work. For I am Kryon, and I know you, and you know me. If these words, or those of past writings, seemed to feel like "home" to you, then it is because your higher self has intuitively recognized the writing of a friend. I love you dearly, as do all entities who are here in service like the Kryon.

Chapter Ten

Questions from readers
about
Self-Discovery

Questions From Readers about Self-Discovery

Chapter Ten

From the writer...

It's time to address some of the questions from the readers of Book One. During the first year of the Kryon book pre-publication (the non-paperback teacher's edition), the letters came steadily from all over the northern hemisphere, asking questions and requesting more information. The following are selected questions written to Kryon by some of those readers about self-discovery, and the implant. I have not used any reader's name, city, country, or even initials, since I have left in some of the personal remarks by Kryon so that you can relate to these compassionate answers. Therefore I feel I have maintained the integrity of the confidential communication. In some cases I have included questions that may seem like duplications. This is because there was so much concern over many of the same issues, and the answers were different enough to give you, as the reader, even more insight as to the true messages from Spirit.

It is also possible there might be some duplication of information in these answers to information contained later in this book, since there follows transcriptions of certain verbal Kryon channellings done at the Kryon "home base" in California before a monthly group called the *Kryon Light Group*. During these verbal channelings, Kryon also deals peripherally with some of the same concepts as those addressed here.

Question: I asked for the neutral implant, but don't know if my request was accepted yet or not. I have begun to experience more vivid dreams, which is very unusual for me, and I experienced depression of a more severe degree and length than I normally have at this phase in my life. Is it possible that these are related to the power of suggestion, or that my guides have left in readiness for the master guides?

Answer: Dear one, the very moment you read that you could ask for the implant, and committed to do it verbally, the changes in your life began. Remember that Spirit knows you, and is not in your linear time frame. This means that we were in preparation for what you wanted long before you asked for it. Your new guides had arrived and were standing by at the very time you expressed the intent.

Intent is honored by the Universe as much as a verbal promise in your culture, and therefore it is the way of things that your request was immediately granted. Do not ever try to "analyze away" in a mental way what your intuition tells you is happening. This will not serve you. You should look forward to more enlightenment, and a wiser feeling about those around you in the near future.

Question: I find myself afraid to go through the negative things that the book said I might. I want the implant, but I don't want blackness and depression. I am also afraid that I might lose my husband as well... and I don't want to. Am I confused?

Answer: If more humans could express their fear verbally, and as you have done in transcription, they would have a far better understanding of their karmic attributes. Let me answer your question in general, then specifically. It is common for the humanness in one to fear the astral, This in itself is a phantom, something that is not as it appears. Do not fear the implant... ever! The implant is the first step toward greeting the higher self, that part of you that has been suspended, waiting to come in to finally greet you and become one. You may have confused the implant and some of the transitions of its implementation with some Earth ritual that asks you to sacrifice something in order to have something. Nothing like this is occurring with the implant. Instead you are being prepared and cleansed so that you can accept mature wisdom and inner peace... and of course lack of fear. Don't mistake this process for any kind of sacrifice! When you clean your body before you put on new clothes... does it hurt? There is no punishment here. Also know this: when you ask for the implant, you are asking for your contract to be complete. This is your perfect scenario, and there could be no better place for you than fulfilling it. The Universe will not give you something negative when it gives you the tool to complete your contract!

Dear one, you are so afraid of being abandoned, it shouts from your very soul. This indeed is your karmic attribute, and is the one that will be voided. You fear being alone without the guides, and you fear the loss of your partner. Understand that the implant will begin to clear this fear. Specifically in your case, when you no longer exhibit fear of abandonment, your partner will know something is different, and you will become a far more stable partner for him. Look forward to a far better relationship when you are balanced, and finally have this karma of fear removed from you. Only those whose partners and mates were specifically there to play out karma will leave, and yours is not one of these. Do not fear the implant. One new guide is already in place due to your expression of intent, and you will have an easy time with the others as well. We love you without measure, just as your human parents were supposed to have done... and did not. Spirit will not forsake you.

Question: I know that I want to call for the guide change and neutral implant, but at this moment I wished that I lived nearer to you so that we could have a counselling session! My fear is that if I take the implant, I may cause pain to my family. I have two children aged 15 and 10. I know I have karmic links with them, and I am in a dilemma, for I don't want to lose them.

Answer: I sat at the feet of a lovely human mother last week in a private channeling who was admonished to "place her children on the altar of Spirit" and have peace. This is a direct reference to the very old story of Abraham and Isaac, where Spirit wanted to give a very strong message for history... that in order to save your children, you must be willing to sacrifice them to God.

The message is clear for you as well: these precious entities will be with you for their time of raising, and they will not be removed from you... if you are willing to raise them under the umbrella of Spirit. In fact, dear one, in your case your change (due to the neutral implant) will affect your children in a positive manner... which is directly in your contract. Instead of losing them, you will give them a great gift that would not be given otherwise. This is the tremendous beauty of how Spirit works. Be willing... and Spirit honors intent (to the letter).

The neutral implant changes YOU, which in turn affects others around you, and makes you a co-creator with Spirit for the things in your life that you need. The thing that changes the most is FEAR. Fear of things that otherwise would send you into spirals of imbalance suddenly retreat from you, and you stand there wondering what happened. You get balance in the process, something your children will see, enjoy, and try to emulate for the rest of their lives. Long after you are gone they will remember how their mother reacted and dealt with events and people... and these things will affect them. This is your contract with the young ones. This is why you received the book. Please be peaceful with this, and let Spirit know (verbally) that you recognize the contract with the children, as you ask to proceed to the next level. Can you see the love that goes into all of this?

Question: I don't want to become a person without emotion. Will the neutral implant make me passive? If I no longer react to the drama of neutralized karma, what is there? Will I laugh?

Answer: That part of you which is human and laughs, and is joyful and loves, is one of the only parts of Spirit that passes to you unchanged when you arrive on your planet. Believe me, your question alone is very humorous indeed!

When you receive the real peace of Spirit, you receive an empty emotional agenda. Understand what this means: this does not mean that the emotions are no longer there; it only means that you are now free to use them without wasting them on karma! No more worry... or fear... or anger. Now you can turn the former drama of karmic interaction to the far more pleasing and positive attributes of celebration, joy, love... and yes, even humor. Especially humor. Are you laughing?

Question: I have children 3 & 6. I am afraid to petition for the implant, since I am afraid of losing them. I am also uncertain what will happen between my husband and me. Although he is not a spiritual man, he is a good father and husband. I don't want to lose him either. What should I do?

Answer: Immediately give intent for the implant. For you, and all humans, know this: the implant is your reward. There is absolutely no sacrifice or suffering involved in this process. Those who leave your life will be the appropriate ones, the ones you are finished with, the ones who are here to complete karma with you. The transition period is difficult for some, especially for those who are deeply involved in karmic attributes. Those like you, who are poised and ready for change, and who realize basic truth when it is presented, will not have a great deal of trouble exchanging guides.

Let me speak of your children. This is important for you to see: the children and you chose each other carefully before you came in. They are yours for the duration of the rearing, as is the case with all mothers. No mother need ever worry about losing children because of the implant. This is not universally appropriate. Even if the children test your limits of temperament and tolerance, it is appropriate, for the implant will adjust to help with this. What happens after they are grown is another story, for then they will have the responsibility to Spirit and karma, just as you do now... and will deal with you then in relation to that. The Universe loves the children as much as you do, and needs you there to take care of them until they get their own enlightenment... perhaps with your help. Look into their eyes sometime and try to "recognize" them. Ask for information from Spirit on this. It is often given in dreams, and may be amusing, ironic and useful to know who they "really" are.

As for your husband: his spirituality has nothing whatsoever to do with what will happen to you if you take the implant. He is loved every bit as much as any human in lesson, and has his own path and process. Your involvement with him, and the resulting children, are indeed part of your karma, but what happens after the implant does not have to be negative. The messages in the first book are warnings of what could potentially happen, so that those with the heaviest karma would be ready. If he is tolerant of your process, and lets you alone in your personal quest, then it shows you that the karma between the two of you is not of the kind that would remove him. Your partnership is very appropriate, based on what happened in past lives, and is not a heavy attribute. Taking the implant will change you, but he may enjoy the change and comment on it, making the partnership better. There is never a need for any balanced human to evangelize the new power, and no human will ever take the implant and make anyone around him "wrong" because the other didn't take it. The resulting wisdom and balance involved in the implant precludes this.

Question: Kryon's description of a key fitting a lock made a lot of sense to me (Book One). Does this mean that if the cause of the illness is discovered and the belief changed, that a new implant is earned, thereby changing the lock and curing the person? Kryon also says, however, that healing occurs in an instant by communication of the higher selves of a balanced individual with a sick one. Does this mean that trying to find the cause is immaterial? Is there then any point to regular 'hands on' healing, and is it possible to self-heal at all?

| Note: See letter on page 92. |

Answer: Dear one, this answer is appropriate for you, and all the others who will read it. It has to do with healing, and has to do with individuality and contracts, and therefore past lives. Without question, calling for the neutral implant will provide for personal healing. It is the fastest way to allow for it. As in the case of the dear one healed of cancer, (see page 92), immediately upon taking the implant, she was healed of her large brain tumor... and it didn't just fade away; it vanished! She was obviously ready for the healing, and her body was just waiting for her intent to be verbally expressed. What power this is, and it is yours now!

The 'key in the lock' message (Chapter Five, Kryon Book One) was a scientific biological discussion that Earth scientists should see, for there are hints for cures there. It is appropriate that you continue your earthly quest for universal healing. This is completely separate from the power you now have to personally heal yourselves... which is from spirit. One is biological discovery for all, and the other is your new personal power.

Spiritually, Earth illness is part of your contract, and reflects past lives and why you are here. You have actually chosen it, for when you are not on Earth, you are planning your next incarnation. You choose the lessons for yourselves, and potentially the solutions, thereby raising the planet's vibration. Remember that there is no predestination. This means that any human has the potential to be healed; no one is hopeless. It is all dependent on how ready he is to accept it. Will it serve his contract to heal at this time, or is there more to go through (including death) before he is finished with it? This is why we admonish you balanced ones to offer the healing.

'Hands on' is wonderful! You should use it for others at every opportunity. Instant healing is also possible, even through one balanced facilitator. Or in the case of one who has taken the implant, it can be self-done – co-created (as in the tumor healing example). It all depends on the personal path of the individual.

Some of you may need to have "new-age" mechanical tools to provide for healing. Since your intellectual side is so resistant to any belief that you could do it alone, it needs this kind of physical assistance. All this is appropriate, for the Universe recognizes the differences in your paths. This is also why all this is so complex.

You can summarize your part of this, however, in what you are to do with the information. Don't try to figure out what is happening spiritually; Make no assumptions. You are to offer healing without judgment. It can be "hands on" in person, or by verbalization in meditation and prayer without the person even knowing about it. Depending on the individual's receptiveness and karmic path, healing or non-healing will be appropriate. Then leave it alone without taking responsibility for negative or positive results... since you are only there to **offer the process, not to accomplish it**. Later I will speak of the difference between co-creation for yourselves through your new power, and the appropriateness of facilitation for others. Your co-creative powers are for you only. Your power of counsel and healing for others is also very potent, but subservient to the other's process... much like these writings can't "make" you do anything, but offer you a great deal if you are indeed ready to believe it.

The Kryon Writings
1155 Camino Del Mar
#422
Del Mar, CA 92014   March 27, 1993

Dear Kryon:

Two years ago I was diagnosed with a large
brain tumor. I subsequently went through
medication that did not work, surgery that
was unsuccessful and radiation treatments
that did not take. The tumor continued to
grow. It was life threatening.

During this time I made a pilgrimage to a
holy shrine. I also received many prayers
and holy relics from well wishers. I repeated every prayer and used every relic. I
used every metaphysical approach. The tumor
continued to grow.

Then in December, 1992, my daughter gave me a
copy of *Kryon - The End times*. What a delight it was poring over the words of Kryon!
On January 5th my husband and I decided to go
for the neutral implant.

By January 21st, with all other tests showing
the tumor was very active, another MRI was
ordered. On the way to the hospital, my
husband and I did our neutral implant ritual,
asking that all karma be gone.

January 26th a very excited doctor called to
tell me, "The tumor was no longer present."

Thank you for printing Kryon. We anxiously
await the next book.

Sincerely,

RN - Thibodaux, Louisiana

Letter received 3/93. This references to the question
and answer on page 90.

Chapter Eleven

The Live Channelings

Kryon
Live Channeling
Transcriptions

Chapter Eleven

From the writer...

In March of 1992, Kryon channeled live for the first time, and the results were published in Kryon Book One. Subsequently, as you can imagine, there have been countless channeled events. Toward the end of 1992, I decided to form a Kryon "light group." This was to be the "home room" for the live channeling work, and so we found a large home in Del Mar, California, the town where I live... and held a meditation/channeling event each new moon.

I decided not to advertise the meetings, or to invite anyone except those whom I knew had books, or had attended once (I took their names for a monthly mailing). In this way I planned to keep the attendance manageable (less than 40), and charged just enough ($10) to cover the room charge and the monthly mailing costs. My idea to keep it small didn't work, however, and In November of 93 we had to move to a church to contain the number of attendees, which grew to more than 100 each month. We stopped the group in May of 94. (We held one more meeting in December for 350!)

Even as I write this for you in 1994, I consider myself a reluctant channel. All this means is that it still takes concentrated effort for me to consider going before a group unprepared. All this practice, and I am still nervous. Kryon tells me that this may never change. It keeps me alert and questioning the validity of what I am doing. If it became too comfortable, I might start putting my own "spin" on things, instead of being in sheer panic and void of plan. Each time I decide to hold a meeting, I again wonder if I should do it (believe it or not). This constant recheck of the importance of my work is something I feel the Universe wants from me... to keep me honest.

One of the amazing things about my work is that it is shared by my wife, Jan. Amazing because all the history of our life together, and the karma of it is now evident... and has come full circle. Jan has been in Metaphysics forever. I think she was born with a tarot card in her mouth! She married me (as a non-metaphysical person) about 10 years ago, and now says that she knew what would happen from the beginning, and was patient with my process until it did. Now she is comfortable letting me take the lead (in the writing arena), while she supports the work. In our live channelings, Jan is always present next to me, facing the people with me. She leads the guided meditations, and adds depth with her music. To my knowledge, right now, we are one of the few husband-and-wife channeling teams around (there will be many more, however).

One of the things this has done for me was to give me a very personal view of what it was to be an unbelieving mate. I did not support her views, and although I never poked fun at them, I thought many of the beliefs were silly and unscientific. All this has now changed, not because I suddenly "gave in" – or suddenly also became silly and unscientific – but because I slowly gained insight and wisdom to understand the presumptive posture of my criticisms. Kryon encourages us to be more discriminating of our human scientific method, and now I understand how limited it is. We wallow in our Earth "truth" of only what we have experienced or can prove. Everything else either doesn't exist, can't exist... or is silly. This attitude prevails simply because we haven't seen everything yet.

The formerly "silly" place of God next to Astrology and Tarot now instead makes sense, since I have been shown the overview. The very thought of this, however, still violates most Earth religious doctrine. Probably just like the last time astronomy was linked to God, when Galileo was sentenced to prison for heresy in 1632 for going against the church, agreeing with Copernicus that the Earth actually revolved around the sun! Back then Earth perceptions were based solely on observable phenomena (very much like now), and the church was convinced that the Earth was the center of everything, and they were somehow able to back it up scripturally. Have we changed so much in 400 years?

When modern Earth science finally gets around to discovering how sensitive our biology is to polarization and magnetics, it might even start to observe what the effects are on human embryos accidentally exposed to different magnetic polarizations, and to examine how "people types" seem to develop (the ones that are so prevalently documented in modern human psychology today). When they discover the correlation between the magnetics and the "people types," they may even start measuring the not-so-subtle effects that astronomical bodies in our own solar system have on Earth's polarities... like the effect of our own moon for instance. This will also expose some information as to why our magnetic field shifted or flipped so many times in distant past geological history.

When it finally happens, this will be the first spark of understanding as to why serious astrology works... and what the actual mechanics are. It will be a telling fact about human nature, that once science sees the possibility of astrology being viable, it will suddenly have credibility... and not because it was a good system that had value... but because our "modern" science now saw how it worked. When astrology is finally verified, I'm certain there will be licenses to obtain for it... and taxes too. The fact that a tax is necessary may be one of the only ways you are certain it is accepted science!

Our light groups in Del Mar have indeed served the purpose of providing channeled information, which I shall present next. The unexpected part of the experience is what I learned about my work, and how it is accepted. Within the same channeling on one evening, we had people changed forever... some even healed, and some who left who still didn't believe any of it. I asked myself how humans could sit though the same experience and come away with such a different perspective of what happened (or didn't happen). Kryon has asked me not to give it energy (easier asked for than done).

When I take my seat on one of these evenings and start to channel the information, I know it is real. I get to feel the love of Spirit, and the compassion often overwhelms me. I started shutting my eyes during these events long ago, since it was very distracting to see the humans as Kryon saw them: all young and vibrant, and loved beyond measure. I get to "live" the journeys that Kryon speaks about. I often feel the wind, and experience smells and temperatures that go with them. Kryon is indeed the love of God. When he speaks of the great "I AM," I get shaky, realizing the immensity of who is feeding me the thought groups for translation. Then I start to ask, "Why me?" Kryon always says, "Because you agreed to it. Now be still, and trust... and let me sit at your feet and love you."

All channelings to follow were carefully transcribed from the taped recordings. Occasionally I altered syntax during transcription to allow for better book reading (*items in italics are post channelled clarifications*). Otherwise, you are "hearing" it just like it happened. As you read on, pretend you are in the room with others. Quite often a sunset occurred during the channeling, bringing the room from full daylight down to candlelight. Del Mar is a beautiful coastal area, and we always felt close to nature. I am told that some of you will be able to "feel" the love that was transmitted during this time, if you ask for it and believe it can happen. These channelings were meant to be read; in fact a large part of the reason for the light groups was to enable the information for this book. The information is for all, not just those in attendance at the time of the channeling.

...Now join our light group.

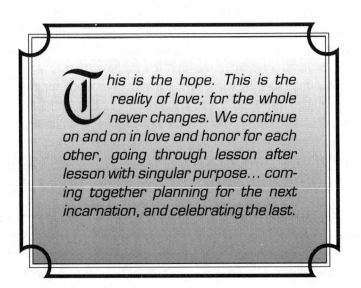

This is the hope. This is the reality of love; for the whole never changes. We continue on and on in love and honor for each other, going through lesson after lesson with singular purpose... coming together planning for the next incarnation, and celebrating the last.

The Phantoms of Karma
Channeling of March 22, 1993

Del Mar, California
Kryon Light Group

The Kryon Writings

1155 Camino Del Mar – #422
Del Mar, California 92014

The Phantoms of Karma
Channeling of March 22, 1993
Del Mar Light Group

Greetings; I am Kryon of magnetic service. I speak to my partner now: I am available to you always, just as I am available to any human at all times.

I speak to an elite group this night. As I have often stated, I am in service to you... and there is great irony in this room, for I sit at your feet and love you dearly. You are the warriors of the light; you are the ones who have chosen to come in and be part of the Earth, to die appropriately, and to come again... over and over so that the Earth's vibration might be raised from this action of your pure love.

And again I tell you that I am here in response to what you have accomplished. The irony and the humor which is in this room now is that the one in the far corner knows the one in the near corner, and vice versa. You know each other intimately, and are glorious pieces of God... such as myself (*even the ones reading this now know you*). But you are in lesson on this planet, and these things are hidden from you completely, and veiled. Your actions are why I am here in this new energy... to make explanations, and to free you from certain life attributes... and to allow for peace where there was none before. This you have freely earned.

Many and great are the badges of color you carry. Those who look upon you in perfect love, such as I, see you in all of your glory. You are all recognized for who you really are: those who have chosen the hard path, those who have chosen to be in lesson on the planet of free choice, for not all planets are this way. Your colors reveal much of who you are. You have no awareness that

I, the Kryon, sit at your feet in service, and that you are the exalted ones. Know that you are loved by us all, and that we know each of you by name.

Even though all this is hidden from you in lesson, there is a full "spark of understanding" that occurs for you as human beings as you awaken each morning. From the deepest sleep to full awakening you are often presented with a feeling of remembrance, a feeling that you cannot explain. There is an instant when you remember who you really are... every single day as you exist on the planet. Your "phantom self" is nudged by a "dream" you had during the night that was worth remembering, something that was peaceful and wonderful, but that you cannot quite bring back to full clarity. This is common to all humans. Perhaps you have experienced it and wondered what it was.

Those of us in service, such as I, are many compared to those in lesson such as you. If you counted the humans in this room, you would have to multiply by eight to have a good idea of who is "really" here now... but the two or three you know best have been with you from birth, and came with you when you arrived... knowing your name. These were assigned to you, by you, and stand ready to create with you when you are ready. I will speak more about this shortly.

Let me tell you how all of this works, dear ones; for although you have full knowledge of what I am about to speak, it still remains veiled and hidden to many of you. For starters I want you to know exactly who is speaking to you now. It is not the human who sits before you; you are hearing the translations of the words of Spirit. I am Kryon. I have never been in lesson. I have come in response to your work. I represent all of Spirit, those who have been here and those who have not... and those who are going to be. I represent the power of love that is from the Sun within the Sun.

I am love, just as you are when you are not here. You know me, and I know you. I see your contracts and your paths very clearly, and I love each of you by name. You sit in front of me in various states of enlightenment and understanding, but knowing there is something here for each of you. I bring good news to all of you. Again, you come here at this meeting on purpose, and the Universe honors your intent. Some of you have come in curiosity, and some have come in pure need; some are here even in desperation. You are loved beyond measure. What we have for you is almost beyond your comprehension.

Each one of you, by agreement and by contract, has come here many times. Through the incarnations of being born on this planet, dying on this planet, and coming back again, you create energy which we call karma. The karma is played out and is acted out over and over, and becomes a set of instructions, or a "play-book" of how your next lifetime will be presented. The attributes you carry now as humans walking the Earth in lesson are a direct response to the things that have happened in the past. I tell you these things because it is necessary for you to know that this "engine" of karma is the most important attribute of why you are here... for this is the school that you have been placed in, so that you may work through these attributes of past expressions.

Each energy attribute of karma is as a daunting black bubble, created especially for you so that you might walk through it, or into it. We (on my side of the veil) call these black bubbles "phantoms," for they may come to you cloaked with fear and terror, or with anxiety. But they are easily voided and "pop-able," and will vanish as the thin setups that they really are. Inside each one is a prize that glows brightly, that will reveal itself upon being examined... and the prize is claimed by walking directly into the bubble and facing the phantom. The prize is that of passing the lesson, or the karma, and having it dissipate and disappear forever from your life's lessons. In the process of the dissipation, energy is released which has been stored for this purpose. The end result is freedom for you and a transmutation of negative to positive for the planet, thus raising the vibration. Can you see how the planet is nothing without you? It is only the arena provided for your karmic work, and now your arena is being changed to allow for power.

Let me explain more about these phantom fears. All of them directly respond to how you lived your past expressions... if you were male or female, if you were aggressive or passive, what you did while you were here, how you died, and the interaction of the other humans in lesson around you. Dear ones, here is a truth to take home in your heart: The Universe does not stand in judgment of anything you have done. It does not stand in judgment of anything you are doing, for you are the pieces of God walking the Earth in lesson, and are responsible to yourselves and the system of karma for what takes place in all appropriateness. Everything you do, however, has consequence. This has nothing to do with cause and effect, or guilt and punishment. There is no such thing in the karmic engine of your life, for the Universe is literal, and sees the things you do as either lessons learned or setups for new lessons to be learned, both of which generate energy of some type.

Let me explain to you, in love, how you should view these phantoms of fear which are specifically your own. Even within this incarnation, the expression of this lifetime, many of you carry anxieties over things which have happened, but that cannot be explained rationally. There are many fears represented here: the fear of being alone, the fear of abandonment, the fear of poor health, the fear of failure, the fear of your own death – all of these are phantoms.... ahhh... especially the last one. The fear of death is so firmly implanted in all of you that it is very difficult to walk through. It is appropriate that it be this way, for if you could see this phantom in all its weakness, you would certainly walk into it... and this would not serve your purpose here.

Some other fears you carry with you are also very real to you. What should you do with the anxiety you feel around those in your lives who seemed to have harmed you? What about the anger you carry toward other humans, and especially those related to you? You carry this "baggage" around with you, and it causes you to act and be certain ways, which in retrospect seem to actually control you. What should you do with this? you might say. This fear is actually one of the easiest to clear! Let me explain.

I wish to give the overview of what is really taking place regarding these anxieties of relationship, in order to grant you the wisdom of a wonderful perception of your phantom. Conjure up in your mind the humans who give you anxiety; make them real before you. Take these who have harmed you in the past: bring them to you, look at them, and then love them for who they really are. Forgive them and watch what happens. They do not have to be before you personally, but the energy of the karmic lesson will be. The first thing that will happen is that the black bubble will disappear. You may claim the prize within, and the karma will be released... gone forever. The second thing that will happen is that with the karmic energy dissipated, these individuals will no longer have an affect on you. The third thing is more obscure to explain, but with the karmic attribute gone, these other "players" on the stage of lesson will actually alter their interactions with you from that point on. Have you affected them? Absolutely. How can they know what has happened? Believe me, the part of themselves that is hidden from them will know it instantly.

Imagine this: what would it be like for you as parents to dress in a frightening disguise and appear in front of your child, and on purpose frighten the child over and over... in love, with the intent of making the child stronger? And then never reveal yourself in the process! It would affect the child all its life, and the child would have a "phantom fear." This would be very difficult indeed! In fact, most of you would never do this, for the sacrifice of seeing your suffering, frightened child would be too much for you to bear.

Yet those on Earth who have harmed you the most, who have given you grief or anxiety and sorrow in relationship, agreed to do so in pure love, by contract with you before you came. They are brothers and sisters in spirit with you even now, never to reveal this while here. When you pass on, you will see them and love them, for the role they played was very convincing indeed! They loved you enough to play the negative role and make you stronger for it. Understand **now** the love it has taken for them to do this, and love them **now** for it. Undoubtedly you are also someone else's enemy, a target for negativity for someone else's lesson... playing the role in a reverse way. How will you feel when this person totally forgives you? Will it affect you? How will you react? The truth is that you will most certainly feel the event; deep within you will be a realization of success... that you achieved the task for the other's good, and you will indeed feel differently toward that person from that point on, even if you never see him again.

Use love as your power source as you do these things. Love those who hate you. Learn to tolerate the intolerable. Be peaceful when peace does not seem to be at hand. All of these things are possible! This is the key to the engine of karma. Those things which you have created are easily undone. Only you have the ability to deal with each one correctly. Tests are created so they may be passed. It is you who authored your own tests, so know this: there is no test which is beyond your knowledge or ability to walk through. The Universe will never give you a problem that is unsolvable. This would not serve any of you, or Spirit. This is a promise to you from Spirit!

Bring your other fears forward and walk into them. Watch the bubbles of karma burst, and claim the prizes inside. With total joy bring them into your reality and dismiss them as the phantoms they are. Do this one by one with purpose and integrity... and wisdom. I speak the truth about these things now, as translated through my partner. Know that the translation is correct even as I am here to experience the words of translation and know that they are accurate... for if it were not so I would stop my partner and tell you so.

Dear ones, it is with tremendous love that I now speak of the greatest fear that pervades at least half of those in this room (*and a great many of those reading this now*). It is a fear that hides, and that most are unaware of, but that is basic to much of the anxiety that is coming into your lives. I, as Kryon, have spoken of this to few, but it is time now to bring it to the forefront. Before I continue, however, I wish to take you on a journey.

Many of you will relate to this journey; and as I take you now, I take my partner with me. I ask him not to feel the anxiety of this experience, since these journeys are very real indeed for him. He must live this journey in order to see what is being shown. The translation of a journey is by experience, and not by thought group. The Kryon sees time all in the "now," and therefore these things are happening now. The linearity of your experience on Earth has been provided for you, but the reality of time is far different than you are used to. I am able to give my partner these experiences in reality, since I will actually take him to the event as it is occurring.

I take you now to a time before the ice. I take you to a great city of enlightenment, and I ask you to view the building you are about to enter. Many of you will feel the feelings and smell the smells of this familiar place. This is a great double-spired structure;

but one of the spires points Earthward, and one points skyward, with the room of action resting between the spires at the midpoint. The structure is supported by legs, or stilts, attached to the midpoint. This structure is familiar to many of you even now as you visualize it through the descriptions of my partner. It is a sacred place of work.

This is the Temple of renewal, or rejuvenation.* For it is here that humans of choosing undergo a three-year cycle of refreshening, the process which will keep them alive and balanced far beyond the years of life that you currently experience in your culture. This is a temple because it is recognized that the balance of a human is one that involves reverence and respect, and honor for spirit, mind and physical. This culture understands this. It also understands the numbers, and the biology and the physics surrounding the numbers. This was the only culture on Earth that easily put them together to create the mechanisms for life extension and for health.

I take you personally to this place that you might again witness the process. As you enter the spherical room you can see the architecture and the designs within. There is reverence for the structure of the twisting ladder, for you can see the designs on the wall for the element of the four, repeated over and over in the series of the three... which gives honor to the work within.

There are two tables in this room. There are many gathered around one of the tables, putting their hands on something which will not be revealed at this time, for it is not appropriate. The "target" human lies on the other table in the room, and one female facilitator stands over this person. You will also notice that both tables are rotating. Also within the sphere of the room there is rotation within rotation, for it is the motion which is the catalyst to the magnetics which do the polarization. Contained in the spire

*See pages 153, 160, 275, and Appendix A for information about the Atlantis "Temple of Rejuvenation."

below the room are mechanics that match the ones contained in the spire above. They work together to facilitate the workings of the balancing engine. Pay attention, dear ones, for even within this elementary description are secrets revealed that you are not yet aware of, but can glean from your hearing (*or reading*) this, combined with your intuitive remembrance of your past. Hold this Temple picture in your mind, and feel the significance of it .

The Temple represents an age where many of you worked, in the place which you called Atlantis. I take you there for remembrance, so that it will help you understand the fear which I will now reveal to you. For your enlightenment in this place and time, and for your efforts of healing in this temple... and for all your understandings of the way things universally worked, and for the resulting long lifetimes, it would seem that you were honored by death. For it was not long after this very journey that you all perished. It was without your understanding that this took place, but there was appropriateness in the event, and it was part of a much larger picture.

You carry with you the seeds of fear around this event. You might say, "I cannot remember any of it; what have I to fear from this?" It is the most basic fear of the teachers and enlightened humans on Earth at this time. It is, indeed, the fear of enlightenment. It is the fear of being healed, and being a healer in the new energy that I bring. It is a fear that you carry so strongly that some get physically ill as you approach the enlightenment and knowledge which is yours. And as you begin to claim the prize which is offered in the new energy, your body rejects it, because it is unaware that it is now safe to claim the prize. There was a time when your body felt this awakening before, and was seemingly rewarded with termination.

I speak of the new energy. I speak of why I am here, and why the new ones in service to you are here. For there was only one other time when we were all here... and you were apparently "punished" shortly thereafter; you remember it clearly at the cellular level. I face you now to reveal that no such punishment will occur this time. These are peaceful, glorious times, filled with potential. You now have the power to move through this seed phantom, just as I have described the other phantoms. Face these fears with me now, there is no reason why you cannot do this.

I speak of the new energy, and I say that I have arrived at your beckoning, for you have allowed for it. You have made the shift. Earth is now primed for something we did not expect, and you are the players. So many of you have asked to be here now, setting your contracts while on the other side of the veil of lesson, knowing full well that this condition had the chance of happening in this manner. You are part of it as you requested! As you sit in front of me now (or read these words), these translations will go into your minds and stay there. They will stick, and you will remember these communications as you move slowly toward the choice to accept them or not to accept them. If you choose to move with the energy, we will honor your intent, and will move things with you in your culture to allow for your growth and power. Beware, however, that if you agree to move forward, you will be taken there regardless of your readiness to go. Do not agree to move unless you mean it.

You have the ability within you now to **create** with your guides... verbally, out loud, anything you wish. Your rooms of abundance and peace and inner essence are ready and waiting. You may walk into them at any time, if you will start the process by verbalizing the co-creation with your guides of the things you need. You can be in places of peace you never thought you could be before. Things which would push your "anxious" buttons would be completely disengaged. You would be of the karmic black bubbles which you carry as your baggage in lesson. All you have to do is ask. This is new, and is offered in love.

I surround you now with the love we have for you, and we wish you to feel it. We wish you to know intuitively by way of the language which is not spoken, but which is being targeted to your third eye even as you receive this message... that everything presented in this communication is true. We wish you to remember. This is indeed your time.

Before I continue, I wish to express again the love that this entity has for your entity. And I wish to tell you that it can be felt through your guides at this time if you wish. When you were children, and were cuddled by your mother, you felt what it was like to have the all-encompassing arms of love surround you. You had no worries, for you were fed and you were clothed, and you were not cold. All of you remember it. This is the way of things now, for we (*Spirit*) are Mother/Father God. We know you by name, and you need not worry... and you need not be cold, and you will be fed. You will have health and peace, if you will simply create it with us.

Finally I give you a parable. You may read into it whatever you feel is correct for your growth at this time: There were two farmers. Both farmers each owned a crop that they were able to farm on their own, without help from others. But it took all their time and they worked hard to harvest it. Both farmers were Godly humans, and they honored the land appropriately. This created a good partnership with the Earth, and they were rewarded with good crops each year, and were able to provide for themselves and their families. Some of their harvest was used personally, and some was sold at market to provide sustenance and abundance. They lived good lives.

One day a human appeared in each of their fields, claiming to have a message from God. Both farmers were interested, and listened intently to the message: The messenger told them that they were dearly loved, and that through their hard work they had earned the power to increase their harvest ten-fold! It was their gift, and they now had the power within them to do it. In order to activate the new power, all the farmers had to do was to purge the old crop that was growing in their fields. They must plow it back into the land completely, leaving none of it standing. In addition, they must search the roots for parasites or fungus, and cast out any impurities they found. When they had done this, they should reseed immediately. In anticipation of their power, the messenger told them that God was changing the seasons, bringing greater sun and rain when appropriate, and shielding them from drought... truly rearranging the components of agriculture as they knew it, to allow for their new gift's use.

Now, it was in the time of year that the harvest of the old crop was almost at hand. Both farmers had tall crops that were ready to cut and be sold at market, thereby giving them their sustenance for the entire year to come, and to allow them to purchase the seeds of next season's crop. Both farmers were hesitant to destroy their old crop, and lose their security for the future season. After all, what would be the harm of harvesting it, then using their power later? This crop, even though it was old, was almost ready, and reseeding now would do no good at this time of year. Any farmer knew that seeds would not grow now.

The first farmer consulted with his family about the message, and asked them for advice. After thinking over what he had heard from the messenger, he and his family decided that God would not bring them harm, so he destroyed his ripe harvest in the manner specified, and plowed it totally back into the land. He examined for all impurities, casting them out carefully, and then immediately reseeded his fields.

The second farmer did not believe the messenger, and prepared to harvest his crop as usual.

Shortly thereafter the rains came. This shocked both farmers greatly, for rain had never come at this time of year before. It watered the seeds of the first farmer's crop, and deluged the standing crop of the second. Then came the wind, where wind never had been before. The first farmer's crop was just starting to grow due to the rain, and so the wind could not take hold of it. What was left of the second farmer's waterlogged crop stood tall, and was easily ripped away by the winds.

And so it was that the first farmer's crop grew to a quantity and height he had never dreamed to imagine, and he rejoiced in his new power to create an abundant harvest... just as the messenger had predicted. The second farmer lost his old crop, and awaited a time where he could align with the new seasons and again plant his seeds, feeling uncertain and anxious over the new uncharted seasonal changes.

Dear ones, what old baggage is it that you carry into the new energy that will keep you from your power? Reach into the middle of your fear and tear out the prize... and move forward with your life. It is time.

As so it is.

Kryon

• For an analysis of this parable, please see Appendix B

Manifestation – Co-creation
Channeling of June 19, 1993

Del Mar, California
Kryon Light Group

The Kryon Writings

1155 Camino Del Mar – #422
Del Mar, California 92014

Manifestation – Co-creation
Channeling of June 19, 1993
Del Mar Light Group

Greetings! I am Kryon of magnetic service. It is indeed easier, is it not my partner, than it was the first time out? For to call on me is to call on Spirit, and that is the privilege of each one who is here. For you, my partner, as a facilitator of the Kryon, I give you the honor at this time.

Each one of you who is here tonight is here on purpose, and the message that you will hear this evening is the first of its kind. For those who are reading this now, this is the first time this message has been brought forth – for it is now time. Through this discourse and the giving of this information, and this logic and this reality, you will hear the truth revealed.

Know this my friend, my dear one: for those seated here this night there is magic. I will explain this more toward the end of this time. Each one of you is known by me, for I represent Spirit. Each one of you is loved by me, for I represent Spirit. Know who is speaking to you now, and feel the sacredness of this! For it is **all** of Spirit, and not just part. It comes from the central sun. It comes from the source of all love and light... and you will feel honored *(in the literal sense)*, for we are here bowing before you. It is the recurring common theme of the Kryon to let you know that you are the exalted ones. We shall repeat this as many times as it takes for you to know that this is so, and that this is truth. For you are pieces of God, like myself, but you have volunteered to be in lesson. You have volunteered to come and to die earthly deaths, with the pain that goes with that process, in order to raise the vibration of this planet.

It is for these things we honor you and we love you. It is for these reasons that you find yourself "remembering" in times of slumber... your trips to the cave of creation, and how some moments, triggered even by events that you share now in this room, bring back memories for you of who you really are. This is appropriate, and this is the goal. For even though you are in lesson, we encourage you to know who you are when you are not here... and that the end of your journey on this planet will bring about a joyous celebration with all of those you have known through the ages. This night something special is happening even as I speak to you. More on this shortly.

I wish to tell you about your new creative power. I wish to tell you who you are, and what you can now do. Before this, however, I wish to love you personally. I wish you to feel the arms of Spirit around you. I wish you to relax in this, and in all the information to come. For those of you who will be "put off" by this, I ask you to be tolerant, to receive and not to shield what is presented here by my partner.

In order for me to tell you about your new power – for it is time for this – I must inform you of history. And so I will give you several stories to show you how things were, and in the process I will take you on two journeys for you to "see" how things were... to set the record straight. Then I will tell you how things "are."

Know this: another theme of recurrence that will be verbalized as often as I sit in front of you, and as often as the reader chooses to read the Kryon words – THE ENERGY IS NEW NOW. It is nothing like anything you have experienced before as humans. It brings with it not only power, but change. It brings with it acceleration. Those of you sitting here this night know of what I speak. It has only been in the last 50 to 60 years that you have pulled yourselves up into a graduate status, and changed this planet!

It is because of your work, and the vibrational change due to it, that brings us (*the elements of Spirit*) together now. We are arriving daily. Those like me, who are in service to you, come with great love and great excitement. Most of you reading this and hearing this know that things are changing. You can feel it (*of course*). There is an acceleration of personal karmic events. You are fulfilling karma faster than before, especially with those around you (*by contract*) whom you know to be your karmic partners. Those of you who know of *co-creation* are finding it happening almost instantly. Those of you who understand *intent,* and know how the Universe works with you, recognize the cause and effect relationship you now have. Whereas before you were able to occasionally lift the veil slightly and quickly scoop out the things you needed, now you stand with one foot firmly planted on each side... even though you are in lesson, and will always be as long as you are here. You now have abilities from the gift of these newly earned powers. What are they? How can you use them? How can you feel the love that they bring? How can you *co-create* for yourself, and manifest the things you need? Do not be in the dark regarding these matters. This message will clear it.

Before we do this, however, I wish to take you back to the old energy. You as human beings on this planet have never been able to carry your own essence. That "piece of God" that is YOU when you are not here, in the past has remained a separate piece, stored in separate places through time. When the tribes of the Israelites were wandering, your essence was carried in the Ark of the Covenant. Did you ever wonder exactly what was in there? ... It was YOU. I speak of you now as YOU, for you were not always who you are now, sitting in this room or reading these words. **You are your own ancestors**, and many of you participated in all of the history that you now read about... leaving messages for yourselves. It is with great irony that you dig them up now, exposing your own words and your own actions!

If you had had the ability to examine the body of the dear one who was reported to have touched the Ark of the Covenant – and died for his infraction – you would have discovered that he had been electrocuted. For the essence of your spirit, which was stored for you in these sacred places during the old energy, was electric. It had polarity, and was magnetic in nature. Certainly this does not surprise you now, as it comes from the Kryon?

In the old energy Spirit appeared before you, and with words such as you are hearing and reading now, gave advice and told you which way to turn.... told you what was coming, and told you what to do. And you obeyed your leaders who heard these voices, for this was the way of it. For without the ability to carry your full essence, you were in the dark... moving through lesson, slowly fulfilling karma, but still as the human "pieces of God" of whom I have spoken many times. Let us set the record straight: when Moses knelt before Spirit, he did not kneel before a burning bush or tree; he knelt before the messenger of Spirit. In past channelings and writings I have told you how this appears, for we are entities approximately the size of one of your homes... spinning with magnificent colors, many of them iridescent. This was what Moses saw as the burning bush he described. How else could he have perceived Spirit? But he did indeed hear words, as you are hearing and reading now in full human language of the time – words in the air, heard with human ears – and it was indeed sacred. Moses removed his shoes, much as you have done here this night for similar reasons. And when Moses went back and fulfilled his instructions, something else occurred that you should know of, for it is time you knew of this to set the record straight. When Moses led the Israelites out of Egypt, as he was told to do by Spirit, he led them across the Red Sea (which was then known as the "Reed Sea"). And if you had been there, you would have seen the high cliffs on each side of this body of water... not a sea you could have waded into easily. Moses then looked for a well known landmark, a land bridge that spanned this sea, and the Israelites went across it freely and willingly. It was this land bridge that collapsed under the weight of Pharaoh's troops and machines, drowning and burying them in the waters. I tell you these things now for credibility reasons, so that you can measure the reality of my words – for this is the way it was. In the next Earth decade you will be allowed to discover the remains of the land bridge for yourselves. It is there for your observation... and you will remember my words as spoken at this communication.

These were the ways of the old energies, and Spirit would actually appear to help you. When your essence was not being carried around from place to place, it was stored in the sacred room of the temple. In this place was the essence of YOU that you could not contain yet, for you did not have the earned enlightenment that you now have. Those temples were the magnificent places where few were allowed to go into – where your higher energy was stored. Know this: when the temple is rebuilt again, there will again be sacred essence and energy there, but it will be different. It will not be yours. It will be ours! This is what will change the Earth. This is the plan, and the contract, for then the Earth becomes the "beacon" in the Universe for travelers such as myself to come... and stay. This is in your future if you wish it... but that is not the subject of the message at hand.

In the old energy you were guided by Spirit in a very simple and direct way – verbally, through messengers to your leaders. It was real. The new energy is so different for you, because you still carry the baggage of the old, and you have difficulty understanding and realizing the immensity of what stands before you personally at this time. For within the new energy you have the tools of co-creation. What has changed is that there is no more Ark and no more temples. For now the essence of who you are, that part of you which had to be carried and stored before, is now within yourselves. And all that is now needed is the connection between your human body in lesson, and this new available essence which you carry with you. These are the "tools" we now speak of. These are your tools which you will use to co-create.

There are four items that should be known about co-creation. If you desire to use this new power of co-creation, you must learn these four mechanics.

Intent: If you are going to co-create, and allow the electricity which is Spirit to flow into your human body (*your full spiritual essence to flow into your physical essence*), you must first give *intent* to the Universe that it is so. In order to do this, you must recognize the karma around you. You must either walk through the karma, or call for the implant, for it is very important that you void your karma and be the light body for the co-creative power to take place. This is why the first book of the Kryon, as translated by my partner, had to do with the neutral implant... to let you know the possibility for you to void all of your karma. This is the critical Step One. Know this, however, that once the intent has been transmitted verbally through your guides, and acknowledged by the Universe, you do not have to wait *(The Universe is literal, and honors your intent as though years of work to get it have taken place.)* Your message sets in motion the mechanics that will void your karma, and will bring to fruition situations that might have otherwise lingered in the background of your life. It also brings about a change of guides.

But while all of this is going on, you may immediately co-create... because the *intent* is everything. It is absolute. You cannot undo your *intent*. Be very careful before you verbalize it, for things will happen to you, and for you, in love and appropriateness when you ask for it. Be aware of what the *intent* is (*how to express it*). It is a quiet time when you speak to Spirit, a sacred time of your own choosing when you say to Spirit, "I wish to take my power and co-create. My intent is that I move into *(become)* a light being. My intent is to use the gift of the new energy as appropriate." That's all it takes. *(The 'light being' is the name Kryon gives to those who have expressed the intent, voided karma, and let the full potential of their Spiritual essence flow and integrate into the physical body.)*

Reality: This is the second item of the four. This is the hardest one. As humans you constantly find yourself placing your bodies into a chair, and yet you never consider if the chair is going to hold your weight. This is the reality of the chair to your human mind. Your chair is a tool. It supports you while you sit. The new energy co-creative power is a tool. It supports you while you live. And unless you approach it with the same reality as the chair, nothing will happen.

Let me give you an example of reality, as I take you on a journey of fantasy. It is not 3,200 years ago, as in the time of Moses and the Reed Sea; this journey is only 200 years ago. I invite you, in fantasy, to visit with me the east coast of your own country *(USA)*. When you deal with Spirit and the Kryon, you deal with a timeless entity, an entity that has no linear time as you do. For I see everything as happening in the now, and I see this fantasy as happening now. See yourself walking into a meeting of the elders of a small town on your eastern coast, when your country and your culture were very young, and your religion was very, very intense. Bring to that meeting, if you will, one of your calculation devices which is based on electricity, the kind you may hold in your hand. Present this to those in attendance. Smile at them in love, and in fantasy watch their reaction, for you have brought them MAGIC... and see that they are afraid! And if it were not for the fantasy, and the fact that you can leave any time you wish from this journey... it would indeed be a tragedy for you, for they would call you evil. They would say you were from the dark side, and they would destroy you... all because you brought them your device. You see, this device, or tool, was not their reality. Their culture rejected it, for they were not ready for it. In their minds it was MAGIC, and magic was evil. You can feel the fear around this for them, and the disbelief that it could represent any kind of 'reality.'

Let us examine the object you took. The object in your culture costs less than one day's meals. It is an object of relative unimportance. It is an object that, if lost, would cause little consequence. Is it MAGIC? Of course not. Is it understood? It is. Is it commonplace? It is. If you brought this device into a meeting in your culture today, what would happen? The answer: nothing. For it is accepted; It is today's reality. You are still human... it was only 200 years ago; what made the difference? Aahhh, do you now understand that yesterday's MAGIC became today's reality?

Therefore, the second item in our series of four is for you to accept the new tools that may appear to you as MAGIC... AS REALITY. See them as the chair. Expect results when you use them, and know that they are yours for the asking, for you **own** them. These tools are not something in someone's imagination. But if you approach these things in curiosity and disbelief, they will not work, and you will be frustrated... and these things will not serve you as they were intended to.

Verbalization: The third item deals with the mechanics of the manifestation, and is a recurring theme. It is verbalization. You have given, and the Universe has received, the INTENT message. You see the reality of the tools before you, and now you will verbalize their use to the Universe through your guides, so that you, as a human being in lesson, can hear them for yourselves. Do not discount these details, dear ones, for there is purpose in the verbalization. If you have not heard the mechanics of the purpose, I will now give them to you. It is important that your own ears hear what is presented by your own mouth. Your words go out into the air, and return back into your own minds, minds which are human minds, which hear what you are asking for. And in this process they "handshake" with what Spirit wants to hear from you as well. And so you have the physical body and the astral body hearing the same message simultaneously, and you have a melding of the two minds (*physical and astral*).

I have told you about love and light. I have told you that they are the same. I have, in this very room, taken you personally on a trip to the innermost part of the atom. I have shown you how this invisible power of love actually defines the arcs (orbits) of the atoms, keeping them apart from each other, holding them at bay.... showing you that the "stuff" of which love is made is present at the cellular level, the atomic level, and also at the astronomical level. We have referred to this love as having substance, and being thick. Even as you now feel the arms of the Universe around you, you know that it is so, for it is fluid.

When you verbalize these things, it is when the fluid flows between that which is your essence as a piece of God, and your essence as a human in lesson. This is critical! The verbalization of what you want and need must be out loud. In the old energy you could think thoughts, and they might happen, in the days when you could temporarily lift the veil and scoop out what you could, until it closed again. It was only necessary then to think on these things, for thought is also energy. Now, for your absolute power, you must verbalize as well.

Self-Creation: The fourth and final item is another critical consciousness attribute. You must learn how this works. You may co-create whatever you desire in all appropriateness. If you are clear of karma, and you are enlightened, you **will not** create events that are inappropriate for yourself or others around you. If you are not in this fashion but try anyway, you will not create. When you co-create, **create for yourself only**. Let me explain this; this is a difficult concept. The raising of the vibration of the planet is what you do personally. It is true that there is group karma, group action and group power. It is true that as you are assembled here in front of Spirit, you are a group, but when you use your power, you use it personally. What being here is all about is personal to you, creating for yourself personally. **Do not involve any other human being in your creations, or your power will not apply**. "But," you might say, "How is this so, when I wish to create peace in a relationship, or good things for my children?" I will give you an example of how this works.

Imagine yourself with many other human beings in a tar pit, covered with tar... dirty from head to foot, unable to move quickly from place to place because the tar is thick. This is your imagined state. Suddenly you discover a "magic" tool from God that cleans your body, and keeps it clean even while you are in the tar! You would appear to others to stand out, for you would be different... white and clean, while the others around you are still in tar. So you co-created for yourself the cleanliness. Now, do you think the others around you will ignore you as you walk freely without the tar touching you or encumbering your feet? as they watch the tar touch your body and never soil you? AAHH... watch! They are about to change! The first thing that will happen is that wherever you walk there will be space, for they will clear the way for you. The second thing that will happen is that they will ask you how such a thing was possible. And when they find the "secret tool from God," then each of them will begin using it for themselves, then more will also be "clean," each person creating for himself personally. Now, as you look at the group over a period of time, half of them or more will be "clean." Stop and think about what has really happened. You have not asked for any of them to be clean, and yet the result of just the one, created for the many!

• *For an analysis of this parable, please see Appendix B*

So it is when you find yourself in a situation with another human that you know is not appropriate... which is filled with negative karmic attributes and darkness... and all you really desire is the creation of peace around all this. Then create it for yourself, and watch what happens to the one next to you! For when you receive peace over the situation, you will have cleared the karma (*that allowed for the negativity*), and there will no longer be appropriateness in a continued negative interaction. Remember this dear one: if there are any things between humans that you find painful or troublesome, your personal karma is at least fifty percent of the reason it is occurring. When your personal portion of the karma is cleared, half the karmic reason will be missing, and the karmic contract and the "handshake" to play out the karma will be disarmed and voided. Therefore the person next to you will change. It is also so in praying for your children. Pray and create for yourself, and watch what happens to them, for there will be instant reaction in those around you when you change.

What are appropriate things to ask for? Know this: for yourself you may ask for abundance. In your culture you may ask for an income stream. You may ask for peace, in instances when it would seem there could be none. You may ask for purpose. You can ask for tolerance over situations and things which have pushed your karmic "magic" buttons before, and made you angry... and you will have results. These co-creations are all appropriate, but when you do this, here is a mechanical attribute to know: do not ask for specifics. If you need monetary results, do not tell Spirit to 'have someone pay you who owes you. Tell Spirit what is needed for abundance in your culture for you to exist: then let the Universe find the ways. Make no assumptions about the "hows" involved in bringing the results you desire, for to do so is to limit Spirit. Remember that We (*Spirit*) are literal, and we try to fulfill actuality of represented requests. So you now clearly have four mechanics of co-creation. You may ask for your goals, but do not tell spirit how they are to be accomplished.

It may seem odd, in a culture where you have been taught to sublimate yourself, for you to consider yourself a piece of God. It may seem odd, in a culture where you are seen as one of many, for Spirit to ask you to co-create only for yourself. But the mechanics are marvelous, and the power is immense, for you will be viewed as special, And those around you will drop their karmic interactions, for yours will be void... mute and gone. You see how the interaction plays out?

It would be my partner's wish now to close, but the Kryon wishes to tell you more. You see there is magic here! Let me tell you something that is happening that will stretch your belief. In the minutes you have been here, you have been cloaked in Spirit.. and the love of Spirit is such that if you ask for an apple, you will never receive a snake. The umbrella of Spirit is awesome, and in this timeless space all of you have been given a gift. The first gift, that will indeed feel as magic, is that none of you have aged for 30 minutes. When you present yourself before Spirit, and you void all your thoughts and problems of the day – and when you raise your hands to indicate you receive, to be the forerunners, the warriors of the light in this time – Spirit rewards you. Magic! The tools of the new energy may appear to you as magic, but some of you have been healed this very night! Healed of intolerance... there are infirmities in this room which are now gone, and will never present themselves again in bodies that were previously weak. My partner has been given a vision which he has shared with very few... where great healings take place which will seem like magic. Claim this as your reality and it will be so!

This is what we have for you, as we sit in service and in love for you. This is indeed sacred ground! There is a reason why you take off your shoes. It is the same reason Moses was asked to remove his sandals before the bush that glowed. It is so that Spirit can wash your feet! And the calm voice that speaks to you now from Spirit through my partner is the timeless voice that spoke to Abraham, and to Moses, and to Noah, and spoke through the great master Jesus... and that was present in the loving words of Paramahansa Yogananda. This is Spirit. It is unchanging, it is loving, and it is you!

This is a special time, where many of you will understand what has taken place, and many of you will receive credibility of this fact when you leave.

And so it is.

Kryon

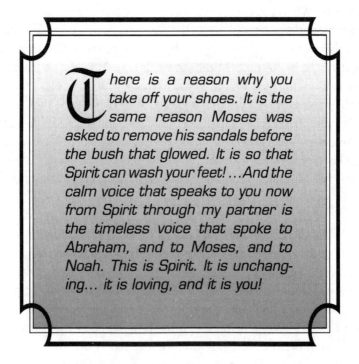

There is a reason why you take off your shoes. It is the same reason Moses was asked to remove his sandals before the bush that glowed. It is so that Spirit can wash your feet! ...And the calm voice that speaks to you now from Spirit through my partner is the timeless voice that spoke to Abraham, and to Moses, and to Noah. This is Spirit. It is unchanging... it is loving, and it is you!

"Don't Think Like a Human"
Channeling of July 19, 1993

Del Mar, California
Kryon Light Group

The Kryon Writings

1155 Camino Del Mar – #422
Del Mar, California 92014

"Don't Think Like a Human"
Channeling of July 19, 1993
Del Mar Light Group

Greetings! I AM Kryon. Do not fear this new feeling, my partner, as I come to you with greater intensity than before. I tell you all now gathered in this spot *(and reading this)* that this is a sweet time, for I know who you are, and you know who I am. It is the recurring theme of the Kryon to tell you that you are dearly loved, and to mean it when we say you are the warriors of the light, and in ceremony and preparation for this time we honor you. For being in this place *(and reading this)* at this time, we honor you... for making the journey to sit before Spirit, when it is actually Spirit that sits before you! Even as I speak to you now, I bring with me legions of entities who have come 'in the door' and who love you. Make no mistake who these are, for they are here in service and help to you, and come in love for you. They come so that Spirit may sit at your feet and inform you of the attributes of the new energy. They come so that they may sit at your feet and tell you how you may use it. How you may be healed, how you may have an extension of your life, how you may have peace. Do not fear the new feeling, my partner.

There is a cone of thickness that surrounds this room, and all human entities present *(or reading this)* may feel it if they so choose. And while you are here in this thick spot, which we call love, you may receive through your third eye area the 'third language.' Even if you were to relax at this time and hear no more English words from this point on, you may read them later, for it is a given fact that they should be transcribed. We wish to speak to you now in the language you understand best. There will be much that transpires between Spirit and you this night if you allow it... which includes much more than the English language spoken here now. Clear your mind, my partner, for what is to follow is important. Let the sweetness of Spirit fill this place.

The ones assembled here *(and reading this)* are loved without measure... beyond comprehension. For you, dear ones, have chosen the hard path, and we honor you for it this night in the form of translation and information, information which will serve you. We ask that you be clear on what is spoken here. Let us speak of the energy – what it used to be, what it is now – and the admonishments of how to use it.

The Old Energy: As an extension of the information presented in this very room last month *(June 19)*, we will review for you what the energy was just a while back. You are in the linear time frame, one step before the other, and this is how the energy was also. Do you recall when you were children, and did not have the responsibility of the house? When your parents left the house, they might have left someone with you to watch the house... or perhaps they did not leave at all, but you did not have the responsibility. So it was in the recent old energy, until just a few of your Earth years ago. You see, you did not have the full essence of 'who you are' with you at that time. In lesson, even though you were pieces of God walking the Earth, the rules stated you could not have your full essence, and the enlightenment level dictated this also.

Channeling: When you sat in front of a channel then, the channel was required to leave her or his human self behind in order to allow the Spirit entity to come forward and speak. This was hard on the human, for it aged the human prematurely. It also exhausted the human prematurely.. and yet the human which allowed for this kind of channeling, did so appropriately, for it was his contract to do so. Entities would come in and speak to you from the other side of the veil, and then they would leave, and the human would return. This was the only way it could be done.

Communications with Spirit: In your communications with Spirit there was no responsibility. It was child-like. Spirit would come to you in a linear fashion and inform you of what was to be, and what was going to happen. Spirit would come and give you rules for you to obey and follow... and you would do so.

Co-Creation: You were not permitted to co-create. Miracles were set up in advance; and even though these actions were responses to what you had prayed for, Spirit had set them up beforehand. You were informed that they were going to take place, so you could structure yourself and know how to feel during the event, and how to have the 'posture' to accept them. Then Spirit would create them for you *(much of this preparation was not realized at the human thinking level).*

Much like the child who was left in the house, you were not expected to do anything for yourselves. But Spirit was there, and you recognized Spirit. This was the old energy, and you have read of it many times. Again, it has only been in the last 50 years that this energy has been allowed to slowly change... and what a change it is! Even as we speak to you now, the legions that I bring with me are here beside you. This is new! They are here in support of the new energy and your new power, power that you have earned!

What is the new energy? This indeed is the difficult part to explain. The entire reason for the Kryon visit, and the time I spend here, is to enable the readjustment of the grid system to allow for your new earned power. I'll explain more of this as this message continues.

Dear ones, this explanation can be complex. It is the task of the Kryon, and the contract of my partner, to try to simplify it during the time remaining. You have an imprint restriction that doesn't even allow you to understand simple time as it really is.

You have an imprint restriction that blocks the understanding of how something could have no beginning or no end. Therefore, how could you ever be expected to understand your own duality... the fact that you are split? There is part of you that does not reside (in you) right now. There is part of you, which we call the 'higher self,' which is stored elsewhere. It was this way in the old energy as well, except that these essences were stored in odd places. You might recall that I spoke in the past of where these places were, for they were in the sacred temples. Now they are stored in the grid system itself.

Now in the new energy, as you take the essence which is 'yourself,' and combine your duality from where it is currently stored and transfer it to your own physical person, you actually 'pull' at the grid system. The energy of your own essence, which is your higher self, is represented as liquid light flowing into your humanness as you take your power – as permission is granted for you to do so – and you pull on the energy of the grid system. Is this such a surprise that I am here to assist this process? This is a difficult concept for you, to believe that there is actually part of you that is not inside you – but it is so. The more enlightenment you allow yourself to have and create for yourself, the more you draw from the grid.

It is important that you know what is going on in the grid system: there is polarity here that you may not be aware of. There is an important storage area in that portion of your continent you call the four corners, which is basically the female polarity. It is being drawn in a fashion which is at a higher rate than the male polarity, which is on the other side of the planet in an oriental area. The humans under this four corners area feel this draw acutely, for it represents a temporary imbalance as you draw from it for your new enlightenment and power. Like a storehouse of energy, you are now allowed to fill your own human essence from your higher self... to let the light flow in and become a 'light being.' Is it no wonder that those under this grid feel uncomfortable? For it is constantly changing and shifting. Those who are female in this area feel it more than those who are male. Those who are male on the other side of the planet, in the male polarity area that is being drawn from, feel it more than the female. And so it is in this new energy that you can take from these areas, for that is exactly what you are now allowed to do. In manifestation that is exactly what you are allowed to do, and in healing that is exactly what you are allowed to do.

The New Energy: Therefore, in the new energy the child is gone. You are filled with the responsibility that is now yours. Can you remember the first time your parents gave you the responsibility of the house ... and then they left? Suddenly there was a seriousness that was not there before. Suddenly there was a feeling of responsibility that was not there before. You as a child were unaware of what was taking place as you assumed your new power... but you felt it. This is the key, dear ones: due to the restriction of your imprint, I cannot explain what is happening to satisfy the desire of your brain which longs for the logic of it, but you are allowed to feel it. When you feel what is happening, you can ask for more, and it will take place. Eventually it will be easy to recognize.

Channeling: Now the channeling is different... just as you hear the one who sits in front of you now, alert and verifying the information as it comes forward, making the channeled information clearer because of this. Spirit may visit you personally because of this... and love you personally because of this. In the past, were you not aware of the love Spirit had for you? It is doubtful you were. Now it can pass both ways. Do you love Spirit? You may openly acknowledge that in your thoughts even now, for Spirit indeed loves you. Let this be a two-way communication, for you now have the responsibility to allow for this.

Communications with Spirit: In your communications with Spirit, things are far different... and this will help explain what is happening. Listen carefully, dear ones, for this is important. The communication is no longer linear. It is as this: when you arise in the morning, do you make a list *in advance* that says 'put your feet on the floor... travel to the other room... turn right or left'? Do you make a list to put on your clothing? No. You use your own intuitive human power of choice to do these things... decisions at the time they are needed. You turn left or right, and make choices to pass from one place to another, you do not need help for this. Ahhh, take note: this is now the way Spirit will work with you, for you are a cooperative piece of God. As you approach life, answers are given through your higher self as you need them, and not in advance. Uncomfortable for you? ... Yes. You must 'feel' what this is like to get used to it, and honor it. Take the responsibility for it *(get used to having answers given as you need them – as an adult, and not as advance information as a child would)*.

Co-Creation: As for your co-creation, you now have the power (as described last month) to create for yourselves. Whereas you could not before, now you can manifest things in your life you need: abundance while you are here, healing while you are here, miracles and 'magic' while you are here. Some of you doubt this even as it is now spoken *(or read)*; such is the imprint you have. Open your heart to this concept, for it is yours.

The implant: While you are here let me speak of the implant, for there are questions even by members of this group about this. Questions have been asked: How can you know you have received the implant? How can you ask for the implant? When do you get it? Do you have it now? The answers are as follows:

Intent is everything! Dear ones, when you have asked for the implant, you cannot turn back... you see, you already have it at that point. Although there may be a transition period while it is executed, the intent alone provided for its arrival. You therefore cannot ask the question 'do I have it?' However, what I am going to tell you now, and what is to follow will help you to understand what to do with it. The symptoms of its arrival remain the same *(as written)*: vivid dreams, periods of sadness or depression. But as my partner spoke of earlier this night, you are all very different. Each of you has a different time cycle; each one of you has come from a different place. Many reading this come from a different culture. Most important however is that some of you have terrific karmic attributes, and some have almost none. The implant is the 'voider' of all karma. It is the reason you are here, to raise the vibration of the planet by way of the 'walk through karma' in order to get on with the work. Nothing raises the vibration of the planet faster than asking for the neutral implant, for the karma is voided as surely as if you had walked through it personally. Those of you with heavy karma remaining will have a much harder time during the transition period than those of you who are almost free of it. Some of you will receive the implant and have no idea you did so! And some of you will go through a period of mourning.

In the process *(of receiving the implant)* some of you will lose negative karmic attributes, and you will actually miss them! There is drama, and you are used to it *(even though it did not serve you)*. How do you know when you have received an implant? Look for the karma to drop between you and the other human beings you associate with. Look how they treat you. Are you aware of problems with other humans in your family? Are you aware of karma in your relationships? When you ask for the neutral implant, these karmic attributes begin to be voided. When they are voided, there is a loss, and the ones on the other side of the karma will feel it as much as you, even though they will be unaware of what has happened. This is the key... and how you will know the implant is in place.

You might ask: once I have the neutral implant, what next? This is new information: you have made a human assumption that your guides' changes were only once. Know this: as you pull your very essence from the grid system and become light beings, your guides will change periodically throughout your life. This will not always be unpleasant; many times it will be joyful. It is part of your growth. It is part of why we *(Spirit)* are here. It is part of why there have to be so many of us to serve you. For every one of you there is an entire army of entities in service to you standing on the sideline and waiting for you to discover your enlightenment to whatever degree you wish to take it.

Now I will give you the basic elements, or the ABCs of the new energy and its use. In the process of this I will make an example... and a parable. This first item in the list is something you may remember from now on due to the fact that it may be humorous to you: Do not think like a human!

Do not think like a human: How can this be, you might ask, since we <u>are</u> human? Is it too much for me to ask you to think as Spirit thinks? Perhaps so. Is it too much for me, however, to admonish you to examine your human thoughts? Perhaps not. Think of this: you are on a road, traveling quickly. Your journey is to the other side of the valley, and in all appropriateness you have asked Spirit to co-create this journey with you. You know intuitively that this has been a proper and correct thing to create for yourself; and so you have created it. You are on the road, but there is one problem: there used to be a bridge on the road to the other side of the valley, but it has been missing now for some time. Yet you continue down the road with full knowledge that the bridge is out.

Do not think like a human. What would a human think at this time? The human makes assumptions. The bridge is not there;

therefore "I will die." "The bridge cannot be rebuilt quickly enough... it was not there last night when I passed the same point!" The assumption is that the human expects the bridge to be as it was before, made by other humans with steel and concrete, in the same place. "My vehicle may not make it if there is no bridge." You make the assumption that your vehicle cannot fly. **Do not think like a human!** Think like Spirit. There is much going on that you are unaware of when Spirit co-creates **with** you.

Make no adjustments along the way out of fear, the second of the three instructions. You see, if you think like a human, you will fear. "What does this mean?" you might ask. It is thus: You are on the planet of free choice, and with this there is no predestination; you may do as you choose. Each time you do something inappropriate, however *(not in the scope of your co-creation with Spirit),* you create karma. So if you fear, and think like a human, what might you do? You might turn left or right on your journey speeding toward the bridge you feel is not there. You may choose to stop altogether. Be aware that if you do, you will again generate karma! Aahh, but you may say: "I have the neutral implant." Aahh, but Spirit says: "Now you have karma again." You just created it. Do you see how this works? Do not make adjustments along the path of co-creation out of fear. **Do not think like a human**.

Take responsibility for the journey. Listen closely, for this is the important attribute, the third in the series. It is thus: if you think like a human and fear like a human, you won't have trust, and will blame Spirit for what may appear to you as a negative situation. "Here I am on the road, speeding to my death! Spirit you have deceived me! Spirit you have betrayed me! I will surely be dashed into the canyon below!" If you take responsibility for the journey, then Spirit cannot do anything 'to you.' You are Spirit! You are co-creating on the road, thinking as Spirit thinks...

unafraid, knowing that where the bridge once stood there will be something to replace it, without assumptions of what it might be.

As you speed toward the valley, suddenly you see ahead of you just what you thought: the bridge is indeed still missing. It couldn't be rebuilt by humans in a day. Aahh, but what is this you also see? There are other humans on the road waving you on around a curve to an area you never saw before... where there is a new bridge! a bridge which took a full year to build! A bridge which was under construction long before you asked for it or needed it! It is wider than the one you expected. It has lights to show the way at night, and speeds you across the valley to the other side far faster than even the bridge that used to be there. It was being built completely out of sight all the time, and only presented itself now... when you needed it the most.

If you understand this parable, you will understand what Spirit has for you in this new energy. Time with Spirit is not linear! Dear ones, we are building the answers before your questions! We are co-creating before you ask. We may do this in all appropriateness, since our time is not as yours. Again, do not confuse this with predestination. You are on the planet of free choice, but we have the advantage of knowing 'in advance' of what you will need in your time line. The setups are in place now for what you will co-create and manifest tomorrow... for healings, for abundance which is coming your way, for partnerships which are around the corner. The setups have started now for creations among you that have not even been conceived by you yet.

A Journey: Now I wish to take you on a journey, and with this we will close this session. I wish to take you to a hot place many thousands of Earth years ago. It is in the fall of the year in this hot area... next to the Mediterranean Sea, inland from the City you call Gaza. Here we find a man prone on the ground, groveling in the dirt. He sits before a messenger of Spirit. The messenger glows brightly... as a fire. The human is the one you called Abraham, and through the channeled writings of the old ones, you should recognize him. Spirit is speaking to Abraham, but he pretends not to hear. When Spirit leaves, Abraham gets up and goes about his business, as though he did not hear, hoping Spirit will not return. Again a day later Spirit revisits Abraham, and again he finds himself prone in the dust. For you see, in this time and in this place on Earth in the very old energy, Spirit appeared to humans far differently, and humans feared Spirit because of it, But it was appropriate. This time Abraham listened, and heard the message, and it put fear into his heart. Spirit told Abraham that he should take his beloved son Isaac, the one born as a miracle from the dormant seed of his half-sister Sarah... his chosen son, his miracle son. Spirit is telling him that the boy is to be taken to a high place and sacrificed as a burnt offering.

Abraham is mortified, but he fears Spirit; you see Spirit is reality to Abraham. He has seen the miracles many times and he knows that he must obey. Isn't it ironic that I take you on a journey to the old energy to exemplify the new? You will see the similarities of trust and humanness in both.

Abraham's heart is heavy, but he assembles two young man servants and sets out for the high place they then called Moriah. It took several days to reach the base of Moriah. All the while Abraham was thinking and fearing... "My special miracle son, born of the dormant seed of my half-sister Sarah, was brought here only to be sacrificed." And he wept.

The three day-trip up the side of the high place called Moriah was not physically difficult, but slow due to the age of Abraham, who at this time was beyond his 100th year, equivalent now to a human in your culture of 60 years. Abraham led the way so that the others would not see his tears, for the trail was wet with them. He spoke silently to himself, and wrenched his hands: "God, why have you betrayed me? ... Why my miracle son, born of my beloved Sarah?... How can this be?" And Spirit said to Abraham, "Abraham, you are dearly loved.... Abraham, do not think like a human.... Abraham, do not fear what is ahead." Although Abraham feared Spirit, he loved and trusted Spirit also. And so he was strong for a while, and the second day he did far better, letting the younger ones lead the way up the mountain.

The third day was the most difficult, for Abraham again had time to think about what he thought was taking place, and about visions of taking his son's life. He thought about leaping to his death, but knew that Spirit would not allow it... or would at worst save his life so that he would have to return to this spot again with the same heavy heart, to learn the same lesson again. It was at this time that Abraham hated his life the most, and wished for it to stop. He had resigned his contract, and Spirit knew it. And Spirit said, "Abraham, dear one, do not think like a human. Fulfill what is at hand with joy."

Abraham got to the place where Spirit had told him to go, but he was so ashamed of what he was about to do that he asked his helpers to remain at a place that was not in sight of the offering area. Again, Abraham's mind was so filled with fear that he could only hold the vision of the blade passing into his son's chest. So he made certain that only he and God would see it. At the altar, his son, who was 9, asked where the sacrifice was, and with total control Abraham informed him that he was the sacrifice. Isaac willingly climbed onto the altar in obedience to his father, whom he loved and trusted.

And as the story goes, at the last possible moment, with the knife drawn and the words of ceremony spoken, Spirit came to

Abraham and said, "Abraham, you are honored for your faith; your lineage will be great, and your trust of Spirit will be told throughout the ages." And then a ram was provided for the real sacrifice, sparing Isaac.

Had Abraham understood the true role of Spirit, he never would have let his humanness take hold. Again I tell you that Spirit will not give you a snake when you are creating an apple. It is not in the consciousness of Spirit to trick a human, or to deceive a human or to betray a human. We support you in love. Through the ages this has never changed, but your ability to understand it has. Now you have total power to do something the Universe never thought would happen; to create while in lesson, to have the knowledge of Spirit love while in lesson, and still hold your imprint. You now have so much more than did Abraham, but you must learn to use it.

Dear ones, the admonishment of love is that you trust spirit as you would yourself. Do not engage in assumption and fear as you co-create with us. Disengage your humanness and trust for solutions you cannot possibly know of, for that is our part of the contract. This is a sweet place tonight, one where there has been much transferred in many ways. Have peace over the next steps in your path, and use your power for it.

And so it is.

Kryon

Attributes of Health & Healing
Channeling of August 17, 1993

Del Mar, California
Kryon Light Group

The Kryon Writings

1155 Camino Del Mar – #422
Del Mar, California 92014

Attributes of Health & Healing
Channeling of August 17, 1993
Del Mar Light Group

Greetings; I am Kryon of magnetic service. I honor my partner's request this night (*to be slow and deliberate... and to wait for him to speak before I continue*). But there is great excitement here! There is sweetness in this place! The sweetness is caused by the humans present here. I would not be Kryon if I did not tell you again and again that I come to you and **sit at your feet**... for I love you dearly. It is the phantom of lesson that allows you to doubt this, and it is the phantom of lesson that would have you think that I am greater than you. For you are exalted, and I have said this many times; but you carry the badges of color of lesson when you are not here. That is to say that at the time you depart this planet, you will wear another band, as a tree does on your Earth, which shows you have been here yet again. And by your colors all in the Universe will know that you are the warriors of the light. You are the special ones who have agreed to come in and die repeatedly over and over, sacrificing these times for Spirit. It is a story you will hear as many times as you come before me, for it is a story that is important... more than you know at this time... and so I will continue slowly.

You have an invitation this night (*and at this reading*) to be filled. Do not worry about the knowledge, for I have instructed my partner to transcribe all that is spoken, and make it available. You may be filled with Spirit, you see; I AM Kryon; I represent Spirit in its entirety. I represent truth. I represent the same truth that was Abraham's. I represent the same truth that Eliyahu had. Through the ages, it has not changed. I speak with the same voice that Spirit spoke with long ago, and I am here for you now representing the same love that has presented itself through the eons. I love you dearly, and I invite you to "feel" the third language, which is presenting itself even now to you. I invite you to be filled with Spirit... to know that you are whole, to know that you have a "higher self," and to be peaceful with all of this knowledge. I come to you at this time both in person and on the pages you are reading **in the now**. For although these words are spoken to my partner, and translated to you "now" in this room, the time line for those of you who are reading this for the first time is also your "now." Which one is the real "now?" Do you understand the timelessness of the Kryon, and of Spirit?

I have never been human. I have never walked, so to speak, "in your shoes." However, I know of your psychological restrictions, for it is my specialty. I know humanness, for it is my specialty. I know how you feel and what you think, for we have adjusted this many times for your "lesson." It is a specialized thing that we do, just as your specialty is that of being in "lesson."

I wish you to know the following. For all of the healers represented in this group, and reading these words, what is to follow is not designed or presented to *mandate a* change in anything you are doing. If you are receiving results in your work, then there is enough said! What is to follow is meant to enhance what you are doing. If you make any changes whatsoever, they will be positive ones. They will be enlightened changes. They will bring greater results! None of the information presented will "make anyone wrong" (*or make any good process wrong*).

Here is something you should realize and understand: **The truth remains the truth, regardless of what you choose to believe**. This means that the truth of Abraham, and the truth of Eliyahu, has remained the same truth through the eons of time. Therefore, the only variable in this scene is **you**. You are the relative aspect. The truth has remained static. Why I tell you this will be clearer as this translation moves forward.

I wish to bask a moment in the love I have for you, for I have brought with me those who will sit next to your guides and speak to them lovingly of who you are. There is excitement here any time the Kryon is allowed to sit in front of those such as you, or have these messages read by those such as you. (*Remember, you are in the "now" as much as those who were at this channeling*). There is great sweetness in this room.

Disease & Imbalance: I wish to speak to you of disease and imbalance. Know this... a very important item, something that must be said for those still doubting what they are seeing: Spirit does not **give you** disease and imbalance! Spirit does not judge you as a human in lesson. Spirit is not here to give you negative punishment; there is no such thing. We want you to know where your **dis-ease** comes from. The answer is something many of you know already, for it has been written and translated before. It emanates directly from YOU; it is your choice. You see, you agreed before you came in to create it, or to allow for it. It is based upon logical judgment and past-life karma. Therefore you are **responsible for it** in every way. Spirit has done nothing "to you." It is yours intrinsically, just as your arms and legs are. You have asked for it in advance, and now here it is. It may seem odd to you that you would – from a different posture while you are not here – ask for something so seemingly negative, so frightening, so fear producing. Is this not in total agreement with the lessons of karma? (*as channeled in March of 93*), which are also frightening and fearful? For this is all tied together. What you have in the infirmities of your biology is simple karma. *It is the body language of your humanness in lesson.*

Let me now tell you some of the attributes of the human body that you may not be aware of.

Polarity: I wish to tell you of the polarity of the organs. Dear ones, when you go into your "modern" medical facilities, nowhere do you find where someone is measuring your organ polarity and magnetic balance. Nowhere will you find where someone is adjusting it. Yet this organ polarity and balance is critical for your health! (How can your scientists miss this when they can measure the electricity of your muscles and your brain? And when they can map the wiring of your body and see the results of synapse in your biological thinking? All this is magnetics!)

I have previously told you in a channeling session of the "couch of your magnetic field" that you "sit" in, that I am responsible for. I have told you that without it you would surely die, for it was designed and created for your biology. I have told you that space travelers must carry it with them or they will also surely die; and yet this is still not acknowledged or understood. The polarity of your human body is a "handshake" to the polarity of the Earth. If you are perfectly balanced, and the polarities are correct, you will not let disease in. The "key" will not fit in the lock (*as referenced to the chapter on healing in Kryon Book One*). Therefore it would behoove you to find out about this polarity! Each organ has its own polarity, which is interactive with the organ next to it. There is complexity here, for there are two kinds of polarity: there is absolute and relative. The absolute polarity is like a dipole, that is to say that the positive and negative alignment remains the same regardless of the physical inclination of the human. The relative polarity is that kind of polarity which changes with the inclination of the human. Two of the main organs have relative polarity: the human skin, and the brain. All polarized organs will respond to the polarity of the planet, and the relative ones will also respond to the physical inclination of the human.

Polarity can be measured for health reasons. It is not a mystery how this is done. You have known of it for 15 or more of your

Earth years. It is measured through the fingertips... no surprise to many gathered here. The device which can measure this is currently available in the country on your planet you now call Germany. I could digress, and tell you more about this Germany. Let me only say this, something many of you have suspected: Germany is a place on this planet which has some of the strongest similarities and attributes common to the time before the ice, in the place you called Atlantis. Atlantis, you may recall, had some of the highest channeled science ever known to mankind... existing next to slavery.

Those who have this polarity measuring device in Germany are encouraged, if they are reading these words, to bring the device out and let modern medical science test it. It is time.

Some of this information may seem silly or unscientific to many of you. The truth remains the truth regardless of what you choose to believe. (*How long ago was it that you didn't believe in germs?... Washing was silly before surgery. The truth of your health remains constant. Only your acceptance of it has changed truth from silly to actual.*)

Motion: More on the polarity of the human being as we continue. The next action which is critical to your understanding is **motion**. When your Earth animals are born, many of you observe them with awe, for they have instincts and intuitions that seem to defy who they are. They know of their predators. Fresh out of the womb, they know where to hide. They know where the food is, all seemingly without any learning... a "remembrance" so to speak. (*Some of them also feature magnetic navigation, a direct marriage of the biological and the Earth's magnetic field... at the molecular level.*)

Listen dear ones to this: OBSERVE THE CHILDREN! ... Spirit wishes you to observe your own human children. When they first arrive, they contain some of the instincts and intuitions they have brought in *from previous Spirit knowledge*. The imprints and the culture around them are not yet developed to show them anything else (*that is, they don't know any better yet*). One of the first thing children wish to do as soon as they are mobile enough to do it, even without the ability to walk, is to SPIN. This is no accident. Watch them. Why do they do this? It is because intuitively they know it is for balance of the polarization of their organs. When they are mobile enough to stand and run, what do they do? They hold hands and go in a circle! (*Observe which direction they take!*)

Some of these things may seem childish or silly and unscientific, but they are truth. Motion is critical to balance. The direction of motion has purpose. I will tell you about it, and then, for those who are skeptical reading this, I will describe why it works... for it is time you knew of these things. If you have motion of spinning to the left (*counterclockwise*), above the equator, or zero parallel, this is a gentle nudge for your polarity. That is to say that it is a "gentle spin." It is good for health, and retains balance. Above the zero parallel, a right movement (*clockwise*) is for healing, for there is far more energy developed through this right spin direction. What I am telling you now is opposite for those on the bottom – that is to say, your bottom – as you view your Earth on your maps below the zero parallel. "Why is this?" you might say. I will tell you... slowly. (*Cosmic humor in this, since my partner is methodical in his process, and wishes the thought groups to come in logical packages in sequential order... or he gets confused and tries to speak too quickly, fearing that the information may be lost and not repeated. A humorous reaction to Spirit, indeed.*)

You have polarity. It is measurable. Some of it is in the form of simple dipole, that is, plus and minus, as in a magnet. I have told you that your body has this essence of polarity, even measurable and visible through your aura. Your aura is the sum and difference of the polarity, and changes with the balance and health of the individual. I have told you that the magnetic field of Earth is the "couch" that you magnetically sit in... that you enjoy, that tunes you, and allows for good health and enlightenment. Answer this: What happens on your planet when you take an iron bar which is magnetized, and you move it in a repetitive motion over and over and over within the lines of influence of another larger magnetic field? You know the answer all too well, for you use this phenomenon daily... or the reverse of it. For it creates energy, which you call current. And because of the fact that you use this daily, you cannot deny it exists. You are polarized beings, spinning against the lines of influence in the Earth's magnetic field, which you must also admit exists, and is measurable. There is energy created by your spin. There is current, and there is balance. Above and below the zero parallel it works, not necessarily because of the rotation of the planet, but because above the zero parallel there is a positive influence of the giant dipole, and below is the negative influence. This is the reason why it works. Motion is the catalyst to balance! How many times have you gone into your healing facilities – your modern science – and they have asked you to spin? There is knowledge here! This is practical information. It is time. (*Motion alone will not work without intent. Please see "bias" under "New Medicine" on the next page, for more explanation.*)

Top & Bottom: Next for you healers, I will tell you of something that will help you in your work: Consider the human being to be polarized. When you choose to lay hands on the human, or if you choose to use your hands, but not touch the human, do so in a fashion which represents the knowledge of dipole polarity. That is to say, use both hands on both sides of the human, top and bottom, front and back. Consider yourself polarized as the healer, passing the energy through the one that is the target of the healing. You will find that whatever application you are using now in regard to this will be enhanced. This also means a possible redesign of your healing tables. It is important that the individuals lie in such a fashion that you be able to touch them both front and back, without their lying on your hands. This, then, is the top and the bottom of it!

New Medicine: You will see some medicines and mechanicals coming your way which are very special. Let me inform you about them. New age medicines will be those medicines which contain life, life that is either currently alive or has been. Here is where the "bias" of the healing comes in. Intent is everything, and is the catalyst for many things. This is not new information, for it has been channeled for you before. Even as you SPIN, intent is necessary for you to create balance or healing. Now I will tell you that as you administer the new medicines, YOU MUST GREET THEM. There must be intent. There must be responsibility. None of the new medicines which truly contain three dimensional science will work without this. You must greet them and love them. If you stand idly by, fearful of them, hoping they will work – letting them enter your body, letting them take over something you should be participating in – they will simply lie dormant. You must greet them (*for them to work at all*). Some of the things I will tell you here will sound silly and unscientific. The truth remains the truth, whatever you choose to believe.

New Apparatuses: There will be apparatuses coming your way which you will also have to greet, for they will not work unless you are in total cooperation with them. This is a new kind of science, where the human being is <u>interactive</u>, a term which many of you already understand.

Healers in General: Now I wish to tell you of some of the attributes of the healers on this planet. This will include many of you sitting now in front of the Kryon, as well as those reading this in their own "now." A true healer, one who is getting consistent results, one who has made it his/her life's work, carries some of the heaviest karma on the planet. A true healer has a long time cycle, does not change easily. Many of you find yourselves also in full retention. Retention means that you retain much of what spills over in your healing. You carry this in many ways: some of you carry it in weight. Some carry it in anxiety, in worry for the planet. Many of you, the true healers, have the phantom anxiety that there is no time left! Seemingly there are so many to heal, and so little time. Many of you are fearful of losing your power. These are all attributes of true healers... planet-wide. These are the ones that are not disturbed when they receive calls in the middle of their sleep from humans in need, who will willingly dress themselves quickly and go take care of "business."

Their heavy karma has created these attributes. You are all trying to make up for something that was created for you earlier. You, of all the humans on this planet, have the greatest gift from the new energy. With the taking of the neutral implant, or even a calling of a new guide, the gift you receive is great! The gift you receive is the fact that you can now walk among those who are dark, among those who are troubled, among the worst balanced humans, and touch any of them, and you will never have any retention again. You need never worry about absorbing their unbalanced attributes, even through physical contact. This is the new gift through the neutral implant. This is the new gift of the guide change. It is part of your new power. There will be those of you who deny this, and you will go to your grave worrying. Those who accept it will know of what I speak.

I must also tell you this: I have previously given information to you that those with the heaviest karma will have the hardest time with the guide change. Therefore, you should expect some heavy times. If you choose this path, you will be honored greatly. Imagine healing without any anxiety or worry! Imagine the fully balanced person... that you are! Is it cosmic humor that gives the planet's greatest healers some of the heaviest karma? There are good reasons, for you are doing the heaviest work.

The Appropriateness of Healing: Now as my partner has asked, I will tell you about the appropriateness of healing.: It has two parts. I wish to tell you of the appropriateness of self-healing, and of that for others.

My partner has asked the question many times, "Why is it that I stand before these who wish to be healed, and I pray for them and lay hands on them, yet there is no result?" Remember this: the disease "belongs" to each human. Your body has allowed it. Therefore you are responsible for it... and you are also responsible for its departure. Therefore you will allow for it to leave. On a personal basis (*self*), it is easier to heal yourself than to heal others, for you are in full control and are fully responsible. Healing can be instant and total; It can be instant and partial. All of these things are appropriate *depending on your karmic path at the time, and the timing of the healing.*

In the new energy calling for the neutral implant (*for yourself*) and the new guides can provide for quick healing. Some of you will have reversals (*remarkable healings*) that will mystify science. Some of you will have miracles! This is where magic and miracles reside; it is with self-healing. These are the things which will be notated and documented for others to see... and the others will also desire the same thing. Self-healing – you are in control of your own karma! Once it is exposed, there is no chance for it to be a phantom any longer. You will know of it. Exposing it and walking through it will heal your body, bring you into balance, and create a situation where the "key" no longer fits the "lock." And I speak now of the disease that is trying to get in.

There is complexity, but basically here are the rules of healing others: Dear ones, NEVER STOP TRYING! When those come to you crying in pain, or those come to you sick even with deadly disease, or those come to you with seemingly mild infirmities such as anxiety or an elevated pressure of blood, do your best and use your process for them. Understand that they are polarized. Use your new medicines and your apparatuses. Teach them of the intent, and do your best to provide for their healing. Here is what will happen. Through your process, and your exposing their karma for them, they may see the light you provide. It may be revealed, and they may heal themselves if it is appropriate. However, their karmic contract will always win! You are not responsible for their contract! You are responsible to turn on the light when they have been in darkness and imbalance. If they choose to spring up, run around and dance in the light, and be healed, it is their choice. If they choose to keep their eyes closed to the light, it is their choice. If they choose to see the light, but be fearful of it, it is their choice. All you are responsible for is to illuminate. Turn on the light and do your best. Do not take responsibility for their healing or their non-healing! Take joy in the process, and move on.

But let me give you this admonition: do not give up! It could only be the difference in one day between the potential human who is going to die and the potential human who will receive enlightenment and live. Who knows, he or she may even read a book that night (*more cosmic humor for my partner*)! When the human is ready, the healing will occur. Part of your healing may simply be to prepare him for someone else to heal. Dear ones,

I do not have to tell you this, but I mention it anyway so that the pages will be complete. There should never be competition between healers! Let the egos be sublimated. Move forward as a group. Use your processes, although they may be different, knowing that one may prepare a person so that the other might be successful. These are the mechanics of healing. For the healer who works over and over with humans, and they die anyway, understands Universal appropriateness and timing. It may be that the dear one was scheduled to pass on just so that he could have the reward of coming back fresh and new... quickly! Is this such a bad thing? (*Your human cultural predisposition of death does not always understand or agree with the Universal "highest good."*) Try to have peace with the appropriateness of Spirit.

(*Can you see the fine line between personal healing and healing for others? Your efforts actually can cause self-healing for others. Since they are responsible totally for their own healing, you actually do not heal them at all. You are simply there to expose them through your healing and balancing process to the truth of their own individual process. This is why the "intent" attribute is so critical.*)

A Revisited Journey: And now, let me finally take you on a journey. It speaks highly of the new energy that the journey we take is one we have taken before. I told my partner that we would do this. I wish you now to come back to the place we visited five months ago. Only this time I am allowed to speak of what is happening. Dear ones, I could not tell you these things five months ago! It was not appropriate... and now it is. Can you see what has happened in this time? Can you feel the power increase? Do you feel the urgency? Do you feel the speed up? You should. This is indeed a sweet place!

I take you to the Temple of Rejuvenation* ... a time before the ice. A time that some of you do not wish to experience again, a time when some of you died. But during this time there was great science. How ironic that it would now "raise its head" again. For now you get to have the same science, but this time without the fear of termination. Pass this fear, for it is a phantom! Visit with me again, this beautiful Temple of Rejuvenation. See the temple clearly in all its beauty, and understand the celebration involved in its use.

Here is where the humans are repolarized! Here is the description. As you stand off at a distance and view this temple, you see a spire pointing to the sky, and a spire pointing to the Earth. It is girded in the mid-point and held up with five legs at an incline. The color is black. The reason? Most of the walls are made up of a composition that cannot be magnetized. There is no metal as you know it. In addition, most of the composition is smooth and light (*doesn't weigh much*). Some of the composition is made from crushed crystals. Remember this composition, for this is the same material which will shield you in flight (*space travel*).

The five legs are hollow. They are inclined to the center area where the work is done, and attached there. The first leg contains the power, running from the ground up into the apparatus. The second leg is also hollow, and contains the entrance and exit for the facilitators. The third leg contains the entrance and the exit for the priest for that day. The fourth leg contains the ENTRANCE ONLY for the one TO BE healed and rebalanced. The fifth leg contains the EXIT ONLY of the one who HAS BEEN rebalanced and healed. You have heard me channel the message that Spirit enjoys ceremony. Spirit enjoys ceremony for reasons you are not aware of. Spirit does not wish to be worshiped... hardly! Spirit knows of your humanness, and ceremony breeds repetition. You see, the truth is the truth and is static. It works the same, over and

*See pages 107, 160, 275, and Appendix A for information about the Atlantis "Temple of Rejuvenation."

over. It is unchanging. Ceremony is the partner to repetition. (*It overcomes the human trait to always want something new. It helps provide for the same needed process to be repeated accurately each time. It often cloaks accurate, truthful processes in the veil of religion. If you had to think about your own breathing, you would have given it up long ago.*)

There is symbolism in the entrance and exit only of the one to be healed, for the entrance represents ascension, and is the color of death. The tube coming back down, which is the exit from the chamber, back down to Earth, represents the rebirth, and also is of the appropriate color. Ceremony and symbolism at its finest (*more cosmic humor*).

I take you now to the inner chamber. Whereas before I gave you the view of what was taking place, I will now tell you HOW it is taking place. There are two tables, both of them are rotating. You will now see that both tables are in perfect synchronization. That is to say that when one turns in one direction, the other does as well. They also turn at the same speed. At one table, I told you previously, there is a crowd of facilitators surrounding the table with their hands on something. I also told you that the target human, the one to be rebalanced, is on a table alone with only one facilitator. Now I will clearly show you what is taking place. At the table with the crowd there is one who stands out. She has her hands on two globes (*she is the priest*). The globes are connected to the machinery, which is humming with great activity above and below, housed in the spires. The spires represent the dipole of the machinery − that is to say, the positive and the negative. The machinery is measuring the one who has her hands on the globes. There are indentations in the globes for her fingers. Those who stand around her provide her with more balance, for the same reasons that those assembled here as a group provide more balance for each other than any one can do alone. The Priest for the day is the one who has the highest balance available... as measured by the machine. The machine measures the balanced organs of the human (*including all the correct polarities*), interprets it, and flows the information into the giant machinery above and below the target human... thereby rebalancing the polarity of the target human's organs. Do you have this picture? Do you see how the polarity works? Do you understand what is happening? A balanced human, with the correct polarity will not allow disease. A balanced human will live a very long time. This is why they called it rejuvenation.

The table which contains the target human goes into many physical planes – vertical, horizontal, and also tipped at an incline (*yawed*). The one who stands next to the target human is a worker, who is only there for the human's comfort, *and to make certain that the human stays firmly in the table's containment system.* The work is being done with three-dimensional science, with the interaction of the machine and the human balanced priest giving the machine information to balance the target human. When the rejuvenation is finished, the target human arises from the table, and there is great celebration. All in the room are filled with joy, and applaud the process. There is ceremony, and a special robe which is worn, and then the human descends down the tube of rebirth to Earth. (*The robe is worn for three days to let all know and celebrate with the human.*) Now you know what has taken place in that temple. It is indeed a temple with a Priest... and it is pure science *(biology and mechanics in partnership with intelligence).*

Some of these things sound silly. The truth will remain the truth, regardless of your level to understand it.

Finally I will close with this. It was two days ago that my partner asked a question. This is a question the Kryon has never been asked before. The answer from the Kryon was insignificant. The question was quite telling.

You see, when Spirit appears before humans, humans react in an expected way (*this is appropriate due to your duality*). Many are fearful. Many are filled with awe. The questions of humans to Spirit remain the same: "What shall I do?" The humans ask, "Where shall I go? – how does this work? – what is going to happen?" Seldom if ever is the question asked, as was asked of the Kryon two days ago. The question that was asked: "What can I do for YOU? What makes the Kryon happy?"

Dear ones, this question alone shows the duality of the love. For you are now able and available to love me as much as I love you. It is the beginning of the two way-communication that we so dearly desire. The new energy is starting to provide for it, and Spirit is starting to feel it, and is responsive.

The answer to the question? It's just what you might expect if you know me.

What the Kryon wants is just to sit at your feet... and love you.

And so it is.

Kryon

From the writer...

Shortly after the channeling you have just read was concluded, I was approached by a gentlemen named Mark Wonner. Mark is a licensed architect who had read the March 93 transcript of the Kryon channeling, and had attended subsequent ones. He was intrigued by the "Temple of Rejuvenation" in Atlantis that Kryon had taken us to twice within several months.

He asked if he could render it, since the journey had been very real to him, and he believed that he had "seen" it along with some of the rest of us. I agreed that it might be nice, and was secretly wondering if he could really "peg" it (draw what I had actually seen). I gave Mark no more information about the Temple as I had seen it in channeling than what was said by Kryon (that you have just read).

In a week Mark called and asked me to come over and see the pencil drawings. As I drove to Mark's seaside home along the coast, I revisited the morality of my actions... for I had not revealed a major architectural point that I had "seen" in session, keeping it hidden as a "fleece" for proof that others saw what I saw. I do this frequently, still clinging to that human part of me that shouts "prove it" when Spirit gives me bizarre information... like a Temple of Rejuvenation in Atlantis.

Twice Kryon had taken us to the Temple, and I felt myself standing outside of it, and then inside of it. I looked at its height-width perspective (aspect ratio), and later I got to actually smell what it was like inside. I suspect I usually get the best view of these things (more than others in the meeting); but Spirit always tells me that these things are not proprietary, so who knows? The information I chose to keep secret was that the two spires were twisted or "corkscrewed" like one of those frosty cones you get at the ice cream store. I told no one of this, and since most church spires are straight in our culture, I expected most people would envision the temple with straight spires... unless they had "seen" what I had seen as channeled though Kryon. Our culture also tends to build "angelic" structures high and slender, like a finger pointing to God.

I walked into his house, knowing that if the spires were not twisted appropriately in his rendering, I would know that Mark was guessing. When he pulled out the drawing, I was astounded! There in front of my doubting eyes were the twisted spires I had seen. Mark had been there too! Why should I doubt these things so much? Perhaps if Spirit beats me up with the truth on a regular basis, I will "get it" some day?

I congratulated Mark on his work, and asked if we could include it in this book. The drawing on the next page is the result of his work. It is my opinion that this is an accurate drawing of the Temple of Rejuvenation that many of us used in Atlantis. At this juncture I know it to be so. Look at it for a while, and see if you have any kind of remembrance of this structure. It should stir something in you, for it was a grand symbol of our victory over death, and our wise understanding of how science, health, and spirit are forever linked... something I long for in these "modern" times.

Here again is an example of how each of us is used to complement the whole of the work. I'm not an artist, and without Mark's willingness to do what Spirit had obviously desired of him – to be at the right place at the right time – we would have no rendering, and this book would be less than it is.

My thanks to Mark, and others who have, along the way, contributed to the work of Kryon. Appendix A in the back of this book contains Mark's full question statement to Kryon about the drawing, and Kryon's channeled answers.

The Writer

Temple of Rejuvenation

Mark Wonner, Architect 1994
PO Box 763
Cardiff, CA 92007

Atlantian Temple of Rejuvenation as Channelled by Kryon
(see pages 107, 153, 275, and Appendix A)

The Entities Around You
Channeling of September 22, 1993

Del Mar, California
Kryon Light Group

The Kryon Writings
1155 Camino Del Mar – #422
Del Mar, California 92014

The Entities Around You
Channeling of September 22, 1993
Del Mar Light Group

G reetings! I am Kryon of magnetic service. I speak now to my partner: have peace with what is to follow, for you may put away yourself, my partner, while the information flows freely.

Greetings dear ones, (*readers especially included*). I know you, and you know me. It is all that Spirit desires at this time to come before those who would gather in the name of Spirit, and let Spirit sit at your feet! We welcome those who are with us (*non human*) that we have not spoken of before... from the Solar group. We honor you, and we love you as part of the support, and we recognize you.

It is the theme of the Kryon to say this each time we meet: that although I AM the mechanic, and have come from a very long distance, the theme is love... and the theme is you, and the theme is your power. We as the Kryon ask to sit at your feet and to love you, and in the process to inform you. Tonight this phrase may take on a special meaning... and you have heard it many times from this channel: YOU ARE THE WARRIORS OF THE LIGHT. It is your purpose while you are here, and it is no accident that you chose to be here (*or reading this now*). Young ones, hear this: it is no accident that you are here either... for I speak directly to you. Even though you may not remember (*or understand*) all that is said this night, there will be an "awakening" when it all comes back, for you will be here (*on Earth*) through the special times (*upcoming planetary changes*). There are no accidents for any of you. You know me, and I know you.

We take this moment to love and greet you, and to recognize the power you have within your higher self, and to recognize your struggle for enlightenment... which is becoming less of a struggle all the time.

The reason for tonight's channeling being what it will be is that humans are naturally curious. I understand you, for it is my job with the magnetic grid, and the magnetics involved in this system, to support you, along with your health and your enlightenment. I know how you think, for I understand your imprint. We have spoken of this many times. Your imprint is that which restricts your knowledge of your own duality, and keeps you "in the dark" until you are ready to express intent toward the Universe to make things different.

Your curiosity has led you to ask about the entities around you... about the hierarchy that is your support group in the Universe, about the other channels that you hear, about the information that is coming in regarding beings with strange names. How does the Kryon fit with all these? Who are these? What are they doing? What should your reaction be to them? Although it plays almost no part in what you are to do with yourselves now in the new energy, I will conform to your request for answers... within the ability and appropriateness I have as the Kryon.

Human beings enjoy placing things in boxes and labeling them. They arrange their boxes carefully, and when they are happy with their arrangements, they move on. I honor this process, for it is part of the human imprint. I hope to give you some labels for your boxes this very night (so that you may indeed move on).

Look for the proof of what is to follow in these next few minutes. There will be some information given which seems like puzzles. Spirit wishes you to put them together. Spirit enjoys having you open your boxes and mix the labels... and find a new label. Spirit wishes you to discover answers for yourself, using the solutions which are all about you. So tonight's channeling will indeed be informative, but there will be unanswered questions. Some of you will have the answers even as you hear this (*or read this*). Others will discover the answers as you read and hear things from channeled information yet to come. You will then remember some of the information given this night, as both read and heard. Look for the proof, for it will be all around you. This information given now is accurate and true, for you sit in front of Spirit. You have removed your shoes in honor of Spirit, and Spirit removes its shoes in honor of you. You are the honored ones. This is your time. It is indeed the recurring theme of the Kryon that I bring to you, and will continue to bring until the time you are no longer here.

Human History Limits on Earth: You have a splendid lineage on the planet! Your lineage goes back as much as 300,000 years. You would be well admonished, however (if you must study the history to know who you were), to look at the information that is only as old as 100,000 years. The reason for this? If you consume yourself in the search for knowledge and information that repre-sents a period longer than that, you will be studying humans which are not like you, for there was a marked change at that time (*100,000 years ago*). The humans that you know around you now conform to the ones of only 100,000 years in age. Before that there was a different scenario, one that might be of interest, but which will not be discussed tonight. We have spoken in the past of your history before the ice (*in past channelings*), and of the seed biology of your species. The difference is in the DNA. That is how you know of your specific human type. (*Your specific colorful history is channeled very clearly by some of those yet to be discussed*.)

Universal Structure: I will begin with the structure of the Universe, and this structure is inconceivable to you. I know of your imprint, and it simply is not explainable; so there will be a metaphor given later. I will tell you, however, of its shape, as much as I can at this time. It is important for you to know that the structure does not correspond to anything you have on the planet. On this planet humans tend to have hierarchal arrangements of power and control, and regardless of your culture – no matter how democratic, or no matter how much you may feel you have a word in what happens – the structure is still from the one with the most to the one with the least. This is how you see and set up organization on Earth. It is how you have chosen to make it so; and with your imprint, it is not surprising that this is the case. It does not reflect, however, the way the Universe works, for the Universe is not about control and power. With human organization the one at the top is generally the one with the abundance, control and power, and the one at the bottom is just the opposite. This is simply not so in the arrangement of the Universe; and I speak now of the entire Universe, visible to you and invisible to you.

It is arranged as follows... the shape of which you cannot conceive, but it is arranged from the inside out, in semicircles of influence and directorship. Power and control are not words with meanings as you know them in Universal organization. The Universe is centered upon love and purpose, as many of you are now discovering in the new energy. Those who are farthest away from the center are not necessarily the ones who have the least, as witnessed by what is happening to Earth right now! Here is an attribute that I cannot explain to you, but that I will tell you anyway. It is cryptic and will make no sense. As the semicircles of influence and directorship get larger and larger from the center, the outward ones curl back inside and become the center again. This is the shape of the Universal hierarchy... of direction, creation, and love. It is a difficult concept.

Metaphor of The Hand: I will give you now the metaphor I spoke of that may help... for there is a grand irony that within the cellular structure of your own biology are clues to the ways the Universe is organized! We wish you to fantasize so that you may interrogate the cells of your own hand. Strange as it may seem in this fantasy, they will be able to answer you with spiritual wisdom, as well as biological accuracy... and give you truth. So you might ask your hand:

Who are you?

"We are your hand... a specialist. I am a mechanic and serve the whole." *(Note the use of "I" and "we;" this is important).*

To whom do you belong?

Knowing full well that the hand belongs to the arm, the hand's cells tell you: "I do not belong to the arm; I facilitate the whole. For without me, the whole would not be able to easily eat. It would even have a difficult time getting up or sitting down. What is good for it is good for me."

Who is your director? Who is the boss?

"We have none. For what is good for the whole is good for the hand. There is no rebellion, for within the structure there is only love and balance, and appropriate polarity between the parts."

Who created you?

"At the very cellular and atomic level of my structure is energy. We were not always a hand. Someday I will cease to be a hand... and then perhaps someday I will become a hand again. Energy is indestructible, so therefore I always was and always will be this energy. The whole does not change, and the number of parts always remain the same."

This is your hand speaking! Quite wise for a hand...

Are you happy?

"Yes. We have a love relationship with the surrounding parts. There is no negative and no rebellion and no inappropriateness. We are balanced (or always in the process of balancing).

Then you might ask the hand a trick question; you might say:

Tell me of the struggle that is within you!

...(Knowing full well of the defense systems of your own body, and of the purpose of antibodies and immunity battles, and of the struggle that you have been told rages within your veins.) But the hand will smile at you, and say, "It is appropriate for the human body to walk freely on the Earth among the diseases and among the microbes... and among the bacteria which enter the body, which might seem odd. But appropriately, the balanced body has the defenses to neutralize these, to turn the negative into positive, to rebalance itself, to assimilate. It is not a struggle at all. It is a transmutation, an appropriate balancing assimilation. There is no battle at all. I am at peace."

These are questions asked of your own biology, and answers that they would indeed give you. These are also the answers that you would receive if you questioned the parts (entity groups) of the Universe from the center outward. For the hierarchy does not reflect the lesser or the greater, only the organization toward creative purpose (which bends back upon itself, involving all at the center). And now we come to the "whos... and whys."

The Entities Around You: I speak now only of the entities that can regularly "speak" to you. I speak now of your support group in what follows. I will not address or tell you of the entities that may coexist on your Earth plane in what you would call other dimensions... which have no role to play in your lesson or your game. They are unaware of you (or your purpose), although sometimes appropriate or not, in your case, you may be aware of them. How do you know the difference when you meet them? The answer is this: the entities in your support group will know you, dear ones (*an understatement indeed*)! They will know of Earth. They will know of this planet's coming of age, and they will recognize your power (*who you are*). There will be excitement, for all of these know of this place you call Earth in this galaxy. If they do not know of these things, then they are of the other. They are not negative, they are simply not in your support group. Therefore, it will do you no good to associate with them. They will not harm you either. So (tonight) I speak of the ones who surround you... the ones you may have heard of, and the ones who are popular, and the ones you will be more aware of as time goes on. They represent entities who <u>have</u> channeled, and entities who <u>will</u> channel. And I will start with the Kryon, not because of importance above the others, but because as you measure distance, I come from the farthest area.

Kryon Facts: I have told you many times that I have arrived here by design... that I was called here through the acts of 50 years of humans having changed this planet. I come to readjust your magnetic grid system for your health and enlightenment... for your imprint. I come to tell you that intervention is possible now (*from Spirit*). You may ask for implants to void your karma. You may take your power; you may become beings of light (*light referring to the power of the higher self*). You may change the vibration of this planet. You may go to "graduate status," and then communicate with the other dimensions. This is the purpose, and why I am here. But it all comes down to you and your higher soul-self (*no matter how many support entities are around you*).

This is why I am here, and in this process I also bring for you, at your cellular level, a release of love that you are allowed to feel at any time. Some of you have already realized that as you sit in front of Spirit (*or read these words from Spirit*) – especially when you are with the Kryon group or any angel-type entities – that now is the time, even as you listen to these words, to ask for (*to co-create*) healing. Has this not occurred to you? Some of you are doing this even now, and it is why I speak of it... for there is no better time.

I have told you that the Kryon comes from the Sun within the Sun, from the great central area. Here is the theme of the center going outward. Now I tell that it has another name, and one you will hear often (look for the proof). It is the Prime Creative Force. This is where I emanate from. What I do for you now, I have done for others many, many times. It is the love and compassion of Spirit that sends me to you now, and loves you as you sit here... each by name. (*As previously channeled, I am sent by a group you call the Brothers, or perhaps "The Brotherhood." This group has always been on the Earth, and is very, very old. It is the group by which I am directed.*)

What else would you like to know about the Kryon? I will tell you, because I have been asked, "What was it specifically that called you here? Did you just show up, or was there an event?" Yes, there was an event, and for the first time I will tell you what it was. A puzzle? Yes, but not a difficult one: In past writings I have told you of the year in which I arrived. Two years before that, in the eighth month of your year 1987, something special happened which summoned me... for there was an interrogation of the planet from Spirit, to see if the vibration of planet Earth fit the universal plan. A "key in a lock" scenario on an astronomical plane (literally) which asked the question, "Are you ready?" And the planet answered, "YES." For the vibrations which were present in that eighth month of your year 1987 spoke highly of what you have done. That was the summons, and the word went forward to bring them... the guides, the masters, the workers, and the mechanic...

and so I started my journey. Those of you who know of such things will know what this event was... small puzzles for you to put together.

My facilitation of the grid, although complex, will correspond to channeled information. It facilitates what you have called in your culture "the twelfth ray." If you understand what this means, you will know the colors of the rays responding to your chakras mix all together to make the twelfth ray. Is it no secret, then, if I am facilitating this power, that you as a human being will change radically? For it affects all your colors and all your chakras. That is how my grid adjustments facilitate your biology. Now do you understand that the trilogy of God is THE EARTH, THE BIOL-OGY and THE SPIRIT, for my work affects and coordinates all of them. This is the service of the Kryon. This is where I came from when I was summoned, and how I work. Being from the Prime Creative Force, however, makes me love you all the more, for I "see" with clear vision your stripes and the colors of the entities of lesson that you are. You cannot hide them from me. I know who you are, and for that reason I sit at your feet. (*I have also channelled the fact that my support group is here as well, stationed in the orbit of Jupiter. This refers to the orbit path of Jupiter around your sun, not a satellite in the orbit of the planet Jupiter. My support group is on a very large "ship," whose name is within your Earth stories around King Arthur [another puzzle]. There are almost 100,000 entities who are here directly in support of my work.*)

The Galaxy – Your Center Group: Each galaxy has a creative direction... a group which has a name. Spirit rarely numbers anything. Spirit knows all the parts by NAME. It is human to number these things. The name at the center of the galaxy of the group which is responsible to you is yet unknown to you; so tonight we shall call them the Sagittarians. We call them this because when you go outside and look in the direction of the constellation Sagittarius, they are there. For in doing this, you will look toward the center of your galaxy, the Milky Way. (*This is not to be confused with those of you born under the sign of Sagittarius; this is only a directional reference to where this group is located.*)

Arcturian and Ashtar: The ones next in line to these, which are closer to you than these – and which interface with you directly, currently channeling on this planet... you have named in your culture "The Arcturians." (*They have directorship for your area, or part.*) They are closely related, and facilitated by those called the "Ashtar." These are so interrelated that it is difficult for you to tell the difference between them. Their purpose is clear, and in their channelings look for the phrases and the words that will correspond to the Kryon. Remember, "Now is the time." Remember to "Take your power." Remember that you are "Warriors of the light." Their task is to work with the young ones. If you were to ask them directly, they will tell you so. As proof of who they are... that the Kryon knows them, and that they know the Kryon, I tell you this: In past writings I have told you when my work will be complete, and that I will be finished in a certain year (although the Kryon group will not actually depart the Earth ever, due to the on-going service of the grid). Eleven years after the year of my completion, the Arcturians are scheduled to leave also. This is a puzzle. Look for the proof. Put the numbers together for yourself when the information is channeled by the Arcturians, and receive verification and the "ah ha!" experience... and know that you sat in front of Spirit this day, and heard truth!

The Ashtar and the Arcturians are the ones who speak to your Earth governments... not to be confused with ships that may have crashed from other areas of your galaxy, or those beings who perished and were found by your Earth governments, even those which might have been captured. These are not the Ashtar or the Arcturians. The Ashtar are able to move between that dimension which you call three, and the one which is above... which is to say that they have the ability to become visible and invisible to you. They bring you great messages of love. Their main work is for the young ones of the planet, and they freely channel wonderful, helpful information.

Your Seed Group: The ones who walk among you, whom you will relate to the clearest and easiest (you might have guessed, for you know them well), are the ones who love you dearly, and are here to watch and prompt you in love. They must stay at "an arm's distance" lest they show off their science. They are like you; they have biology that is yours. They are your seeds, and are from the "Seven Sisters." They are the Pleiadians. There are none that are closer to you (that do not walk with you daily) than these. They have the ability to walk among you, and you cannot know who they are. They are in your dimension, and they must be careful or their science will spill over into yours... and it is not time yet for this. Ask them, "Why are you here?" and they will tell you it is because of love; it is because "now is the time." There is excitement within this group. They are your seeds! (*They bring information of the way things work around you, from the perspective of beings with the same biology as you, who are enlightened as to what is happening in relation to your humanness... very practical.*)

The Solar Group: As we move on, there are others. There are the ones some of you know in your culture as the Solar Group. These are your so-called Angels. These are the ones who watch you and bring you wonderful information, more actual Universal history than any of the others, for the others are facilitators. Most of the others have Universal and planetary goals at hand, but those in the Solar group are filled with history and practical human information for you.... and are filled with love. (*As previously* *channeled, their gold color will identify them.*) I speak now of names you know as Solara, and the Archangel Michael (*and many more not in your culture*). They love you dearly, as the Kryon does. Look to their channeled information, and use it!

Dear ones, if I have not said so before, I tell you now that you cannot possibly listen to only one group, or one support, or one channel, and know everything. We are specialized. Look for, and consume all of the information from the many, and it will fit together for your puzzle and for your enlightenment.

The Masters:
Then there are the ones who are the Ascended Masters. Their attributes are that all of them have been on Earth as humans. Their task is to return via channeling to give you instruction sets, information that is practical for you to know from their perspective of having been here before themselves. These are masters such as Jesus, John the Baptist, King Solomon, King Arthur, many Pharaohs, and those who have sat in high places of great wisdom. Names like El Morya, Sananda, Mahatma, (*St. Germaine*), Kuthumi (*and many more not in your culture*) are only some among the ones bringing the information for your culture. Listen to their instructions, for they will be specific.

About The Templar:
Much information is being given now from this group regarding the rebuilding of the Templar. For the human who sits in this group tonight, who is most interested in this, take back this information: in all the history of this channeled Templar information from King Solomon forward, much has remained constant. The rebuilding of this structure was to take place in the Southwest area of this continent, in this culture. This is still appropriate, and that portal is now open and ready. Now there is a change: there are four other portals on this continent as well that will also work. The Templar

may be built on any of the five, and if you wish to know of their location, you may find it, for the Hopi nation has channeled this for you. The Templar is the communications center for a graduate Earth. It is the new beacon. When built, it will communicate to the other dimensions. Its beacon will tell them, "We are Earth. Our planet of free choice is now in graduate status; you may now come forward" (and enjoy the library of Earth).

You!:
You may think of Earth as very small in the universal scheme of things, as perhaps inconceivably insignificant within the vastness of the star systems as you view them. Nothing is further from the truth! All the enlightened ones know who you are. This planet is where the excitement is, dear ones, for you, walking in lesson, are the exalted ones! When you are not here, you stand tall and spin with many colors. All who look on you know of your "lesson" status, and how many times you have been in duality. As I have said before, it is like the rings on one of your Earth trees; you show your stripes, and all know of these awards, and honor you in celebration. Your job is a most difficult one, much harder and more honored than that of the Kryon.

Your Negative Curiosity: Now I speak to you of something which might generate fear. Before I do so, let me remind you of your human imprint. It is comical in a way that if I told you, dear ones, that there was something wonderful happening, and something horrible happening, almost all of you without exception would say; "Tell me of the horrible!" You see, you naturally wish to know of the negative. This is because your karma is made of fear! ... and you carry it very well. So you are familiar with it, and you are attracted to it first.

The Dark Ones: Let me tell you of those who seek Lucifer, for they are creating a phantom. The Universe is literal, and without judgment. Those who would stand and ask for Lucifer to come forward will receive gratification, for they will receive what they expect. They will be able to co-create the negative, just as you now have the power to co-create the love, healing, and enlightened power of the positive. Lucifer is the phantom of their own creation and making; but let me tell you this dear ones, and never forget what is to follow in my words. One of you in an enlightened state with balance may freely stand in the middle of those chanting and calling for Lucifer, and you will have total power over all of them! There is nothing on this planet that can touch your new power! Those who would call on the negative are unbalanced, and they do so because of their unbalance. This has nothing to do with any negative entities on the planet. It is something humans do to themselves.

But alas, your hand told you, did it not, that humans are able to walk the planet in free expression. It told you that it may be regularly "invaded," but it told you that it had the tools of balance. So it is on the planet of free choice, for there are several types of entities that are allowed due to the rule and direction of nonintervention... to be with you. Almost without exception, these entities are not aware of who you are. They are attracted to your attributes only. They have no concept of the Sagittarians, the Arcturians, the Ashtar, the Pleiadians or the Solar. They only know of the lower vibration of themselves, and they seek information and answers. There is no conspiracy regarding these against universal principles. They simply want to know... and you are their library.

There are several of these groups. One seeks information about your emotions. To the degree of the intervention rule, they are allowed to interfere with your biology. Therefore there are humans who currently have attributes of these negative ones. Being human, however, walking in the light in lesson gives you absolute power over any portion of this dark attribute. These entities are allowed specifically to facilitate your karma, and are an appropriate part of your lesson. This is to say that any human in this condition may recreate balance on his own... assimilation and transmutation of the negative. If any humans feel they cannot, that the attributes of the negative ones are too strong, they now have the power through intent, and the communication with the guides, to call for intervention via the neutral implant (as channeled before). (*Since the implant specifically deals with karmic voiding, you can see the interrelationship to these dark ones.*) These dark ones are attracted to your emotions because they have none, and they wish to study you, for you have an abundance. (*Emotions are energy, and you are like a beacon to these who seek them. They need to find answers, for they feel their very existence is threatened by the loss of this natural energy.*)*

The second kind are also attracted to you. They also have no awareness at all of your quest of lesson or karma. Even though they have no awareness of your karma, what you do with it actually attracts them, like moths in your culture to fire. Therefore they are also allowed to interact in your lesson. I speak now of the ones who are plentiful here because you actually feed them! ... and you feed them with your fear. Those of you who live in fear are daily feeding these, and they will come back and invade your life, pulling you down, needing more food. They understand that the more fear you are in, the more food there will be. As unbelievable as this scenario may sound (*to many humans*), it is true! You will find them feasting at the feet of those humans who call for Lucifer. They are allowed in all appropriateness to be here, but you have absolute power and dominion over all of these... for legions of these are powerless before one of you. Believe it! It is the truth of Spirit. You have no reason to fear any of these dark ones. We have spoken in other channelings of the phantom of fear. We have spoken before of the trust of Spirit, and how to walk through the karma. Now is not the time to revisit that.   *see page 281

The other dark entities are quite simply explained. They are biological, and are like you. They are allowed to be here from other places in your galaxy. They have the machines to travel here. But simply because they have the science does not mean they have enlightenment. These are the ones who have crashed here. These are the ones, through their mistakes, who have been captured, not the Arcturians or the Ashtar. It is the science of these from other places that is being studied by your Earth governments today.

There is so much more to know about those around you, but I have outlined the major players. Each of these groups is rich in its own history and its own lessons, and how each came to be with you. There is great teaching to be had by seeking their channeled works, and much universal wisdom to be gathered by listening to them. They are all very willing to give you lessons in their lineage... to help you appreciate your own.

Now, dear ones, I bring you to the point of this channeling. I want you to feel the love of Spirit, as I project (*send light to you*). Regarding these I have spoken of: perhaps you have felt intimidated by these faceless entities from all over the galaxy who walk the Earth with you... in the trenches of lesson, competing for space – both spiritual and physical? Perhaps you have been uncertain... fearing them, feeling that there are conspiracies everywhere; not knowing exactly what to do... fearing to sleep, not knowing who is good and who is not? I am here to tell you that all of these from the center outward represent the COMPASSION OF SPIRIT! They are here in support of you! All of them! Even the seemingly inappropriate ones are here for your lesson... on the planet of free choice, in appropriateness of Spirit! (*Remember it is your work in the face of all of these that has earned your new power.*)

On this planet where intervention was not allowed, you have done the remarkable! You have lifted yourselves up, and are preparing to move to graduate status. All of these in your support group I have listed tonight, and all of the channels... and all the information that is pouring in from them is being given in love, representing the compassion of Spirit for you! Fear none of these. Greet them and welcome them by name (*your support group*). Learn about them and know who they are. Feel the "oneness" and the love of Spirit that would allow for such interactions centered around you. Know that each time you hear new messages in channeling, it represents the compassion of Spirit, the very reason Kryon is here this very night. Compassion of Spirit is born within the Prime Creative Force. (*There is no exclusivity in Spirit. Your support is all specialized, with no entity taking precedence over any other.*)

There are those of you this night who cry out for healing, who wish to know more about why you are here. How do you feel knowing that there are masses of these support entities for each one of you, who do nothing but support you in your quest... hoping that you will gain enlightenment, hoping you will hear the message and react, standing by at the ready for your action? Does this make you feel special? Does it give a new perspective of who you are? You should leave this place standing tall. Think of the colors and stripes that are yours when you are not here! Think of that part of you that is represented in the duality of the higher self, which is a piece of God in itself! For it, dear ones, is also from the Prime Creative Force.

The Guides: Now, in closing I will tell you of a group I have not spoken of yet. In doing so, I will give you a journey. These are the quiet ones. You will find very few channelings from this group, for literally they are too busy. I speak now of the guides. These are the ones who are assigned to you at the beginning of life, who stand next to you and hold your hands, and love you. These are the ones whom you occasionally feel, but who seem just out of reach. These are the ones who appear in your dreams. It is the cosmic humor of Spirit about dreams, for you can experience other entities and messages in your dreams. You may even directly speak to Spirit in your dreams... all very real and accurate, and appropriate. When you awaken, however, and tell other humans of your dreams, they are just dreams... discounted as fantasy common to all. (*Dreams are often the vehicle of guide communication.*)

A Journey: Angenon and Veréhoo were guides. Angenon was different, for Angenon had been a human before, so he carried the stripe of the human. Veréhoo had never been human, and had always been of the guide group. Both of them had been with humans lifetime after lifetime. Both Angenon and Veréhoo were excited, for they were on their way to another planning session that marked the beginning of yet another human's life.

They were going to meet their assigned entity shortly, one of the ones who was the guardian of the love... one of the ones who would be sent to the Earth plane as a human, one of the ones scheduled to be a warrior of the light. These two guides, Angenon and Veréhoo, standing side by side going into the planning session, were going to meet the entity we call "WO." We have heard of Wo before in a previous parable channeled one year ago in this very room, where we walked through a lifetime of Wo's when he was a man, and we experienced a journey with him where he walked through his "house of lesson." Wo stands now in the chamber of planning, close to the portal leading to the cave of creation. Wo stands ready to pick up his essence and return with his karma intact to the planet Earth. Angenon and Veréhoo are part of the planning. Here it is that Wo and all the others plan the karma that is to be generated from the lessons they are to have... and the planning is clear, not to be confused with predestination.

For again, Wo will come into the Earth plane where he will be exposed to the appropriate karma, and have his chance to walk through it (*just as he had in the past*). This is done to give Wo a chance to raise the vibration of the planet through his efforts, to be recognized by the galaxy... and the Sagittarians, Arcturians, Ashtar, all the way to the Prime Creative Force, for they all know Wo.

So Wo is prepared in this planning session to pick up where he left off (*karma-wise*), and return to Earth. Here Wo plans with other entities yet to come into lesson... and also, dear ones, there is planning with the higher souls of those already on Earth walking in lesson. Karma (*as described in past channeling*) can be a very complex plan. So it was that Wo decided to come back with Angenon and Veréhoo this time as a Woman. And so Wo was now a she (a *WO-man*). The guides willingly begin their journey to come to Earth with her. So it was also that she chose the attribute to be born on the first day of the month of September. She is going to have a difficult time with control!

In the first years of life Wo is abused by her father. Wo is abused by her stepfather. Wo is even abused by her stepfather's brother. By the time she is eleven, she carries the heavy karma of a long time cycle... by design (*and during this time Angenon and Veréhoo stand beside her, watching the karma of choice develop*). Dear ones, there is no such thing as predestination. Your lessons are decided and set in advance, but the solutions are yours while you are on Earth. It is thusly: if you were to send entities down to Earth as hammers, and visited them some years later, you would not be surprised to find them in the company of nails. This is logic, not predestination. So the attributes of the ones who are born September 1 are known, and you will not be surprised at the problems they encounter, or the lessons they must walk through.

Wo has a difficult time with males. She has no problems with abundance, for this is not the karma she carries. Money seems to come easily to her, and in the area of Earth business she delights in her quest to rise to the top. She becomes spiteful due to the anger and energy of her karmic lesson, and devours the spirit of males around her... enjoying the game of business, and of winning over her male counterparts. She tried partnerships three times, but none were able to survive – due to her anger. As Wo grew older, her health became poor, and her imbalance allowed for over-abundant acid, and other stress-related disease.

Angenon and Veréhoo watched in love, quietly knowing that all was appropriately set for the next stage, for Wo and the others had decided that this could be a very important incarnation, one to remember due to the Earth's new attributes. It was in Wo's 47th year that she was "accidently" exposed to an enlightened woman... in one of those business intensives where humans are forced together for a week, unable to escape... in the name of efficiency. Angenon and Veréhoo both recognized the woman, for it was an entity from the same planning session that they had attended 47 years earlier. This was the one who was scheduled to appear this year, and if Wo was ready, to inform her of Spirit.

As fate would have it, Wo was interested in this woman. Wo wanted to know what was different about her; and as if by fate (*cosmic joke*), Wo approached the woman late one night and asked the questions, "Why is it you have peace? How are you so tolerant of the others? What is your secret?"

Angenon and Veréhoo were on their toes! Poised in the balance of a moment was everything they had waited for. They both sensed the potency of what was happening, and knew that this was the prime window of opportunity that they had waited for. Never in the history of their guide assignments had anything like this happened! As the woman spoke, Wo remained stoic, but taking it all in. Later that night it happened. Alone in her room she openly wept, raised her hands in apparent desperation, and verbally asked if Spirit would grant her an audience. As if the light was suddenly turned on, Angenon and Veréhoo were put into action. She had expressed intent! Yes! The Universe was listening. Yes! there was something else grander than the human intellect, and Yes! she could have peace during her incarnation. Angenon and Veréhoo celebrated... and it caused Wo a very sleepless night to have all that activity around her bed!

Things started changing quickly for Wo. She met with the woman many more times, and became fast friends with her. She met others who took her through processes and gave her information she needed. All the time Angenon and Veréhoo were rejoicing in the new communication they were allowed to have with Wo and her higher God self. A third guide from a master guide group joined Angenon and Veréhoo; and so it was that Wo was able to walk directly into her karma, and forgive those who had harmed her so. And so it was that she gained wisdom, and realized her responsibility for all that had happened. And with the WISDOM came LOVE. And with the LOVE came ACTION! There came a time when Wo not only was able to tolerate the males in her life, but actually partnered with one... successfully and lovingly. Quite amazing.

In Wo's 53rd year, Angenon and Veréhoo were asked to leave. Wo had become of such a vibration that a totally new set of guides was needed to best serve her. As her set of guides retreated from her, for a period of 90 days Wo was without support, and even under this stress, Wo understood what was happening, and quietly busied herself with other human things... and got through this period without difficulty. Angenon and Veréhoo celebrated again. You might have thought that they would have been unhappy, in sorrow and grief to depart from a much loved friend... and at a time they had waited and planned for so long! But Angenon and Veréhoo knew that the parts were in balance, and the graduation of the one exalted the whole... and they willingly departed without rebellion, or even a thought of anything but love for the process.

We leave Wo there, because her future has not been realized yet... much like your own.

Dear ones, so it is that those from the center outward celebrated the enlightenment of Wo, for it was a universal event, and known by all. It was significant, for it helped the whole. And so it is that those at the center of your galaxy knew it, and so it is that the Arcturians, Ashtar and Pleiadians knew it, and all the angels of the Solar group, and the Ascended Masters knew it. **And so it is that none of them together could do what the one did by herself... to give the intent while in lesson to take her power.**

And so it is.

Kryon

• *For an analysis of this parable, please see Appendix B*

Postscript from the channeler

Many times while channeling, I receive concepts and visualizations that are not translated, due to the fact that the information comes very quickly, and some is lost. In past channeling, I have asked for Kryon to slow down so this would not happen. As I become more accustomed to these live events, I know the pacing will coordinate better.

Unspoken, but very important is an underlying feeling I had all throughout this channeling. Kryon wants us to know that if the star player of the game becomes enthralled and stands motionless in awe of his teammates, the game will never get played, much less won. We are to gather information as tools for our own action. We are never to study the members of our support group to the extent that it stops our own development. No support entity has come here to be worshiped, and this is why Kryon gives guidelines about the dangers of becoming a channel "groupie" or a history "groupie," studying those beyond the veil for the goal of historic study itself. This is a pitfall to our full potential, and is not appropriate. It's all fascinating stuff, but when you consider that we already know all the information, and it's simply hidden from us while we are here, the historic study pales in comparison to the excitement of what is **not known**... the future of the planet through the action of enlightened beings such as we! Kryon says (in love): Get on with it!

The Writer.

Earth Changes...
"Your Wake Up Call"
Channeling of February 10, 1994

Del Mar, California
Kryon Light Group

The Kryon Writings

1155 Camino Del Mar - #422
Del Mar, California 92014

"Your Wake Up Call"
Channeling of February 10, 1994
Del Mar Light Group

Greetings, for I AM Kryon of Magnetic Service. Greetings, Enlightened Ones. Greetings, doubters. I know who you are, but you are all loved equally. Let us take just a moment to adjust the room, for the love energy, which is to be transmitted this night via the third language, will accompany all of the information that you also have in your language.

For each one of you right here in this room, there are at least two others with you. They hold your hands and love you and look to you, and ask you to give intent to get on with your lives. Feel the parenting of Spirit and your Higher Self as you receive the information of this night. Feel that you are not alone. Even though you might close yourself in a closet, you are not alone.

The recurring theme of the Kryon in Spirit, dear ones, in this new energy, *is that* you are the Warriors of the Light. You are the ones we serve in love. We are here because of what you have done. We service you. We love you.

There is good news afoot. We wish to tell you this night (both those of you in this room and those of you reading or listening to these words) that you will number in the thousands; for what is presented this evening is new information, information that you have earned. Information that some, even within your belief system will scoff at, until the scoffers may someday come to you, shaking in fear, wanting to know what you know about what is happening. Pay attention, for you may be able to help them.

Tonight's channeling will be an answer to a question placed to the Kryon shortly after last month's New Moon. The question was a good one, but it reveals how you think like a human.

Here is the question: "Kryon, it was only a matter of days from when we sat in front of you in channeling, in front of Spirit, when the Earth shook violently not too far from this very place. Lives were lost; property was damaged; there was great fear. Why didn't you tell us? You say you love us, as Spirit does. You say we are pieces of God, and yet you said nothing *of the quake*. How can you sit in front of us," the question goes, "and be silent about something so important to our lives?"

Dear ones, Kryon and Spirit, and the messages from the Great Central Source, do not speak to groups. Spirit speaks to individuals and hearts. And the answers this night to that question will speak to individuals and to hearts, so that you will not fear any of what is taking place. You will have full understanding that with the changes of the Earth, you will receive changes in power, that they are commensurate, moving together. One is given, that the other may happen. You are not to sit in fear over these things, but over these things you will have peace because you will understand what is taking place.

Let Kryon tell you this evening of earthquakes... of weather changes, a little of agricultural changes, and of the magma of the Earth. What we speak of now, as Spirit speaking to your heart, we speak of not to generate fear, but to give you good news! When we are finished, you will understand the good news.

Your Earth is changing. It is why I am here, for I have been summoned, literally by yourselves, in the new energy, *to accomplish* these changes. Earth is being prepared for Graduate Status, Dear Ones; for Love and Abundance, for Peace, for the portal to the other dimension. And it will all happen, centered around the next eight years. Things which might not have happened for one or two hundred years will now take place.

We sat in front of you and told you of the acceleration of the new energy just last New Moon. And here we are again, saying it has begun. Those of you who know how earthquakes work will understand how they are related to the engine of the magnetic field, for the magnetic field is generated by the polarity of the engine between your Earth's Core and the Sun. And when Kryon starts to adjust the magnetic grids, other things will take place. This cannot be a surprise to any of you.

We have told you, even in a channeling session of a year and a half ago, paraphrased: "That if you do not wish to get wet, do not live on the bank of the river." You have chosen to live in places where there are known faults in the Earth. I speak to those of you in this room. If this generates fear, then you should leave. Literally, the advice from over a year ago from Spirit was to move where it was cooler. This is not cryptic. This is accurate. If you are fearful of your area, you should leave. For, Dear Ones, it will continue to move, and it will move more! In addition, the Earth will move in places where you never thought it would move before. Those who feel they are living in complete safety in the middle of your continent of the Americas where the wheat is grown – the Earth will move there. In your desert areas, as they look to you on the coast and say, "I do not wish to live there; the Earth moves." ... Theirs will move as well! It comes with the territory. You see, Earth is under construction!

Let me speak of your weather. Scientists in charge of your weather will tell you that amazing coincidences have happened in this last month, creating very cold weather that is highly unusual. They take into account the things that they expected of your jet stream, of your cloud cover, and they say that the "coincidental" events lined up exactly correct for a very unusual event... for you to have arctic-like weather. Let us see what they say about "things" when the amazing coincidences occur again, and again, and again. They are going to have to come up with another story. We'll see what they do. Yes, your weather will continue to change. Prepare for it.

We have advice regarding those who would grow in agricultural areas. Dear Ones, remember this: you are in charge of feeding the world on your continent. This will never change, for it is as it should be. But there will be areas where you used to grow crops where they will no longer grow. And you will not know why. There will be other areas which were never conducive to the growth of anything which will be fertile. Spirit gives Honor to those in the business of growing food on your continent, for what they have begun. Abundance, two and three times, will be given to those who continue to find ways of honoring the Earth, in natural ways, to control the pests that would eat the food as it is grown. That is to say, those who learned how to use the natural resources of the Earth to do this will be rewarded.

Let us speak now of the magma, the internal fluid of the Earth, for you are going to see more of it. It is only the sensible thing, even if you are not a scientist, to know: that as the magnetic grid shifts, and the Earth moves accordingly and wiggles, as the weather changes, there will be shifts in the Core. Volcanoes will be the result; islands in the ocean that will be new; volcanoes which lay dormant may now be active, and hills which you never suspected were anything but hills may become raging infernos.

We do not say these things to create fear, for within the scope of your human's science, many of these things you will see coming and will be able to move accordingly. So they will not generate fear. The only fear generated will be from those who have no idea what is taking place, and view these things as negative. It is the karmic attribute of the planet at this time to generate this fear. It is the intent of Spirit, at this time, to generate peace in your hearts through the knowledge of what is taking place. You see, Earth is under construction, I say again.

It is similar to having a situation, perhaps as humans, where you have a home remodeled around you. And you have cordoned off one or two rooms to live in while it was taking place. You know what that might be like, for there were noises and rumblings and shakings and irritations and inconveniences until it was finished. And you could hardly wait. But when it was done, and you stepped into it, oh, the smell was fresh, the energy was new, there was the feeling of abundance, of newness. This is what is taking place, Dear Ones, on your planet in the next eight years. This is the reason the Kryon is here: to visit you, to make the adjustments, and to channel the information to you of your new power.

You are not victims of these changes. Let me say that again. Victimization has no part in your life. There are those, even within this room, who feel their lives are being tossed and turned, that they are victims of the waves of the planet. They do not understand their new power. It sits in front of them, with a wall paper thin, with all appropriate love, awaiting to be given. All that is needed is intent. The recurring theme of the Kryon is to ask you to show intent to Spirit. Take your power! Claim the guides that you have, and recognize them. Ask Spirit for co-creation of what you need. And part of what you need is the ability to ask, and to marry to your Higher Self, in order to be at the right place, at the right time, you see. This is critical! For Spirit will never sit in front of you and tell you to turn left or right again. This is up to you. This is your new power – to know, and not for us to tell you.

The information that comes next has the potential for great fear. And it is during this time we ask that you truly feel the Love of Spirit. The information given should be received wholly, and listened to carefully... for it is astoundingly good news.

Let me tell you of an appointment. Let me tell you of an astronomical event. Let me tell you of a dark, ominous rock in space that some call asteroid, some call meteor *(the temper of fire making the difference)*. The rock, approximately one kilometer across, has a name; a name known to all Universal Entities. It is known as "the death rock." It is **Myrva** spelled: M-Y-R-V-A. This black thing is what was appointed to crash into a continent on Earth in the next eight years. And so the scenario went, that it would kick up a giant cloud of dust, besides devastating the land around it. The event known as **Myrva** was to be the termination of your planet. And there were reasons why this would be taking place. The dust cloud would then create the global warming effect. Your ice would begin to melt in your polar caps. The added weight-shift of the water going to other places on Earth, raising the water level of the oceans, would then create a rotation on the axis of the planet, and it would turn. Needless to say, you would all perish. **Myrva** was coming.

I had previously told you when I first arrived, that the Kryon had arrived in the year 1989, that there were three years of preparation before we could begin channeling to you in 1992. We also channeled the information that the support group for the Kryon was in the orbit of Jupiter *(the arc of Jupiter's orbit around the sun)*. A-haa, Dear Ones, there is great mirth and irony in what I am about to tell you. Scientists, listen carefully: You know of the mathematical ratio and relationship to the orbit of Jupiter *(around your sun)* to the path of the asteroids in the ellipse around your sun. You therefore know why we were at Jupiter. Even those in this room already may guess.

For it was the task, in the three years that we were here *in your solar system*, before we started to channel to you, to completely and totally disable **Myrva**. And so I sit in front of you... rejoicing! with the fact that **Myrva**, "the death rock," one kilometer across, is now in pieces. This was not mysterious; there is protocol and precedent to what happened to **Myrva**, for your scientists have seen it before in other asteroid paths. You see, it was a marvelous alignment of many coincidences. *(Kryon laughter)* You'll have to ask your weather scientists what happened; *they seem to understand about coincidences. There was* nothing *you might call* mystical. When we arrived, we set in motion the very things we knew should take place. You have earned this! You have earned this.

Myrva is no longer. And so, although the rocks are still on their way to intersect your planet within the next eight years, there are far fewer of them, and the course has been altered. Depending upon the energy level of this planet in that time, the rocks may miss altogether. If any of them hit, they will measure only a matter of a hundred meters across or less. Something to cause fear, but not planetary obliteration.

This is the information that we wish to give you, the specifics. Your scientists will see it. They will give you reasons. They will not be mysterious or mystic; they will be mathematical. This is how Spirit likes to work.

So, Dear Ones, do you see how important you are? Do you realize what you have done? For all of this was work in response to the interrogation of Earth in 1987, when in the eighth month you were asked and measured, "Are you ready?" And much to the shock of Spirit, the answer was "Yes!" The planetary vibration had raised to the point where we knew you had changed the entire polarity of Spirit!

And so **Myrva** is gone. And the event we called **Myrva** will not take place. Let us now speak of how that affects the Hopi Indian Map, and also clear up what has taken place with the newer map generated by your philosopher, Nostradamus. We had previously told you that the Hopi Map is accurate. Remember this, Dear Ones: we also told you that all prophecy is one hundred percent accurate – for the moment it is channeled... for it represents the energy level of what is to be expected at that moment.

The Hopi Map is amazing. It has information there which is astounding to you. But it is not *the information* that you believe *it is*. For the part of it that was channeled, which represents the water encroaching upon your land, accounts for **Myrva**. And I am telling you that **Myrva** is gone. Therefore, the news is even better than the Hopi Map shows, and you can ignore many of the outlines *of the water*. More on this in a moment.

How is it, you might ask, that an old channel can have better information than a newer channel? For Nostradamus was only four hundred years ago, and he channeled **Myrva** also. And he told you that the outlines of your continent would be covered with water, for the very reasons I have given you this evening when I told you what was supposed to happen. But you see, in the last five hundred years of your Earth existence, your consciousness took a dive downward. You used the technology that was given to you for negative instead of positive, for harm instead of good. Therefore, it was the expectation of Spirit that Earth would be terminated, that the experiment would be over, and that the polarity would be shifted in a far different way than it has been.

These were the times of Nostradamus. And when he channeled that (*Myrva*), he knew what would take place in the hundreds of years following. And that was the energy (*of his time*) which he represented in his information. You may throw it away; it is not accurate! For you have changed that, even within the last fifty years of your existence here on this planet. And so the Hopi Map raises its consciousness to be more accurate than that of Nostradamus.

But the places on the Hopi Map that are astounding are the accuracy *areas* of the five portals on your continent which are going to become the communications areas to the other dimensions. These portals are totally and completely accurate. These are the places on any one of which the **Templar** may be built. These are the places for communication to the rest of the Cosmos. Many of you will live to see the beginning of this. Good news, all. Good news. **Myrva** is no longer "the death rock."

You have earned this! Know who you are! Stand in Honor, even though your imprints and your implants do not let you fully understand what has taken place. The news is good!

Now we tell you the answer to the question, "Why me? Why should I have to be suffering through this, and be in fear? Why should it happen personally to me at this time? Why can't you just tell us what is going to happen, and we can steer clear of it?" Let me explain. There was a man named Joe. Now, Joe was a good man, and he lived a good life in your culture, on your continent. Joe lived a peaceful life, for he worshiped complacency, even though he did not know it. You see, Joe did not like change. And in the abundant society you live in, Joe through the years was able to raise a family and to live a good life, because he managed to make "in" match "out." Therefore, he was satisfied. And Joe lived year after year after year with "in" matching "out."

And therefore Joe was balanced, he thought. Joe found himself waking up at the same time every morning and going to sleep at the same time every night. Joe found himself with his family enjoying the same vacations in the same places year after year. Joe had shelves, which he prided himself on, where he stored his records. Every time Joe paid an obligation, he put it on his shelf. Each time Joe had photos and pictures of his family, with the technology which you have for such things, he put it on his shelf... layer after layer after layer, showing the years and years of sameness for Joe. You see, Joe was into survival. As long as Joe was able to make "in" match "out," Joe was happy.

And then came the magnetic storms, the storms of Spirit in the New Energy. There was water; there was cold; there was heat. The Earth shook, and all the things that were on Joe's shelves fell on the floor and he was afraid, for the change was great. And he saw that for a while "in" might not match "out."

And yet Joe, being a man of integrity, ran out to help his neighbors before he helped himself. And he spent three full days helping them, for they were in greater need than he. When he was finished, he came back to his own house with his family. Joe realized something; he had met people who had lived next to him all of his life. He knew their names and saw their faces. He saw that they were much like he was. He saw that he loved them, that there was camaraderie, that they were helping one another. Joe saw that each one of them had a gift for him, something he did not expect: a piece of knowledge, some insight, a hug... some love. And Joe realized the wasted years he had, not understanding or knowing about his neighbors. Joe felt somehow changed by this. He knew he would see them again, and he made appointments to do so.

Joe set about the task of cleaning up his mess. All of the things that were on his shelf were on the floor. Oddly, Joe found himself throwing away much of what was there, and he only put a fraction of the items back on the shelf that had been there. Something that mystified him at first, but then became clear, is that all of the things that he was picking up looked the same. Year after year even the amounts of the obligations were the same; only the dates had changed. He saw his photos as he picked them up and put them on the shelf. The only difference was that his face had aged in the photos. Then Joe realized what had happened; he had spent most of his life in complacency, fearing change and not living to his fullest. Joe realized that he had missed a great deal, and that he had missed a lot of love. Joe realized that sameness and complacency were not good things; that fear was not a good thing. Suddenly Joe realized that he had changed.

And so he called his family together to tell them about his change, that they were not to fear what had taken place, that because of his neighbors and himself, they would make it through. And Joe even told his family that the next time it occurred, they would go to church (*meaning the next time that church was scheduled*). (*laughter*)

You see, Dear Ones, Joe had a wake-up call. This is your "wake-up" call! His (*Joe's*) life had to be stirred a bit for him to understand "wake-up," to see what was around him. This was the service of Spirit, to do such things. And his guides were rejoicing that Joe found a different light to look at... and it was not one of fear. For fear is your human nature, your imprint, and your implant. It is meant to be changed (*designed to be transmuted*). It is meant to be walked through. It is there for you to alter; it is not there to torment you.

There are enlightened ones, even in this room, who will not need to be stirred. And yet there are ones who will. Spirit does this in all Honor and in Love. To not do so would be a travesty; to let you simply remain in the place that you are, without a "wake-up," would not be accurate or appropriate, or loving.

The question is asked, "Spirit, why can't you tell us these things in advance? At least tell us when they (*these things*) are going to happen, so we can move away and not have to experience them." Dear Ones, those of you who ask this question still do not understand: that the raising of the vibration of this very planet is caused by karma, the "walking through" of karma. In other words, the fear, the result of what is taking place, is the action that is necessary to raise the vibration of the planet. It may be a surprise, but your Higher Self can intervene at any time, through intuition, and tell you to step aside.

This is what we mean when we ask you to give intent: to be married to your Higher Self, to let that piece of God speak in your ear and say, "Perhaps it is time for you to move. Perhaps it is time for you to turn left or right,"... to learn to honor the voice, to let your guides lead the way, and to do what is told, out of harm's way, as we readjust your planet and give you your "wake-up" call. This is your new power, and we invite you to take it!

If this were not the case and if we told you in advance of these things then we might as well simply lift the veil, turn on the lights, and let you all go home! This would not be appropriate. You are still in lesson. This is still the Planet Earth, the only planet of free choice. Those words should ring in your mind, with Honor!

Now let me tell you how Spirit perceives your future, the actual way it is done, so that you will not be confused by the apparent enigma in channelings. On one hand, Spirit tells you (*that you*) have an appointment with a death rock which has now been disarmed. It tells you of events which are coming, and will happen, or may not happen.

This is telling your future, is it not? On the other hand, Spirit tells you that no one can tell you your future. It is up to you. It is in your hands. So who is right? Which hand holds the truth, you might ask?

Both! Here is how it works: Spirit has set a portion of your future in place, things representing the fact that you can only exist in the dimension of what you call the three. You cannot exist in any other dimension; this is the dimension in lesson for you. You can not change that.

The planetary aspects of what are around you... you cannot change that. It is set by Spirit. And yet your path within these things is up to you. Here is an example: pretend, if you will for a moment, that you see train tracks before you. Spirit has laid a track out. Spirit knows where the track is going. Spirit knows where other tracks will intersect it. Ahaa, but there is no train, only the tracks. Spirit then gives you the train. You are the train, and Spirit leaves you alone, and says, "You may now travel on these tracks. We know where they are going. We also know what will intersect them, but you have control over your train. You may make it go as fast or as slow as you wish, or change its color, thereby changing its vibratory rate. You may also let it go into disrepair, where it might stop. You may destroy it. You may make it better. You may improve it. All of these things are well within your power."

Therefore, you can now understand how Spirit can tell you about certain things on the track. But it is up to you riding in the train to change those things that are well within your power to do. Therefore, you can now understand how the future is set by Spirit in certain ways, and yet controlled by you in others.

Now we come to a portion of this channeling which you may not understand at all. Dear Ones, again we ask you to feel the Love which is transmitted this night, via the third language. Make no mistake who sits before you at this time. This is Spirit from the Great Central Sun. This is not one Entity who has lived on your planet before, coming back to give you advice. You are receiving the same information, from the same source, as all humans throughout history did. The same Spirit of Abraham and Moses is before you now. Feel the Love that is yours, the Honor that is yours. Sit before Spirit.

One of you is being healed, even as we speak, for you are giving intent. Others of you are considering it. There is still one who is doubting. Feel the Honor, and know that you are Loved, uniformly, regardless of your belief of what is taking place at this moment.

Spirit wishes to tell you now about how it views life, human life, and this is difficult. I'll tell you why it is difficult: it is because your imprints are so strong. All you know is survival. You come into the Earth plane with one prerequisite: that you stay alive! And that is what you think about. That is what you were designed for, and it is correct and appropriate! And yet, this is not the way Spirit sees your life.

This has many ramifications and is complex, but let me give you an example of why you may not understand what is to follow. Imagine that you are very, very hungry. You have not eaten in a week; you are starving. Literally, your life is in danger if you do not find food. Many of you in this culture have never felt this way. Some understand of what I am speaking.

Everything that you do, and every waking hour and every sleeping dream thinks of food: finding it, eating it, and surviving.

Then suddenly imagine yourself in a lecture hall, and the professor there is giving you fine gourmet recipes for food! The chances are very great that you will not remember even one of those recipes, for all you will think about is getting the food.

Your imprint regarding your human life is much this way. Spirit honors the fact that, especially in your culture, you value this so greatly. It is appropriate, for it is your survival.

Remember this, Dear Ones: that before you ever arrived here, there was a planning session, where you planned appropriate Life, and appropriate Death. What you see as horrible, tragic, negative things was planned by yourselves. This includes what you would consider accidental death, even of children. You see, when you are not here, the planning sessions are done with Honor, and with Love *and with the wisdom of God consciousness.* A child may agree to come in and remain a child, only to be terminated appropriately for the parents' karma. You see, there is much of this that takes place. Therefore, there are no accidents; and all death, even that of groups is appropriate... known by yourselves and by your Higher Selves especially.

Imagine if you were going to give a play, and everyone in this room were to decide to learn a part and put on the play. There would he heroes and there would be villains, and some of you would even choose to die on stage as part of the story.

After the play was successfully put on, you would have, perhaps, a cast gathering, where there would be great frivolity. And you would discuss how the play went, and just how well you did. This would not be a time where you would hiss at the villain, cheer for the hero, feel horrible tragedy for those who died on stage. Do you understand the meaning of this? Spirit does not view your deaths as you do.

There is proof of this in your ancient channelings, even of the book you call the Bible. When you read the story of Job, it will surprise you, for Job was an example for other humans. Spirit allowed for the killing of his wife; the killing, some say, by God. Spirit allowed for the death of his children. Spirit allowed for his abundance to be yanked from him.

This was Job, a faithful, faithful man of God. An example was made of Job, for his faith remained steady, and he understood and honored Spirit for what Spirit was. How tragic, you might say, that God would allow such a horrible thing – for just an example. You do not understand the mind of Spirit, and you still don't with your imprint.

I tell you all of this so that you will understand how Spirit looks at life. But I also tell you this *so you can know* that things have changed. The things that have changed are these: with the acceleration of the New Energy and in the next eight years, and with the things that are going to take place, we wish, among all things, for you to remain.

The times for death, rebirth and new karma being generated are gone, if you choose... for it is inefficient now. Things are moving far faster than they ever did before. We wish for you to remain, to marry with your Higher Selves. We ask for you to have very, very long lives. We desire miracles to take place within your body, and for that reason we have given you the knowledge of polarity. Dear Ones, we want you to stay!

Hear these words, among all others this night. That even though Spirit seems to be indifferent to death and termination, it is not indifferent to your heart. We understand what your karma brings, and how fear works. We wish healing for you. We wish each one in the sound of this voice, and reading these words, to understand that through intent they can remain.

Some who have already taken the steps have been miraculously healed. This is documented. This will happen over and over and over, until many of you who doubt will get the picture. We wish you to stay.

If you have enlightenment and know what is happening, and wish to be part of the great plan, it is not our desire that you be crushed by a boulder... or drowned by a flood. We wish you to stay. Reach out to your guides this very night, and take their hands.

Dear Ones, I tell you finally of another alignment, an exciting alignment on April 23rd (1994). April 23rd may come and go without anything being felt, but April 23rd is one of the most astounding alignments with the Hopi Map yet, for it allows a portal of interdimensionality to open.

You have the honor and the privilege of an alignment that will eventually allow for communication to other dimensions. An alignment will take place that will facilitate the catalyst for this, so that when the portals are finally realized and built, you will understand what this meant to be accomplished.

There are those who still do not understand dimensionality. They do not understand that you live in the dimension of the three, and that is all you see around you. There are those who will make judgments on the planet – about life, about spirituality, about Spirit and Love itself – based only upon what they see. And yet there is so much more here than what you see.

What you see is only what you have been allowed to see in lesson. What is taking place right now in this channeling is interdimensional, for Kryon and Spirit live in all dimensions at the same time.

I am privileged, as Kryon, to be with my partner, the channel, all the time. Although this has not been mentioned before, Kryon does not simply appear once a month. Kryon lives with the channel. And the energy of Kryon will remain with him and his Higher Self as long as he asks for it, as long as he is in the integrity of the moment. It will flee from him when he violates that.

I watch him as he views what you commonly call television. When he finds a specific channel that he likes, he stays with it for hours. And that is the only thing he sees; the only reality to him is the story on that channel. Now, if I told him, or others around him, that the channels on each side of the one he was viewing did not exist, they would scoff, for they know that there are many, many channels. And yet there is no evidence of them at all! They do not appear as shadows next to the one he is watching. You see, they are hiding because he is not **tuned** to them.

Dear Ones, you are tuned to the channel (*dimension*) of the three, but there are many *dimensions* around you just as active, just as real. This is the information we finally wish to show your science, so they will understand how it works to serve you.

Spirit is finished this night with the channeling and the information. Spirit is not finished with you! Walk out of this place feeling loved. Is there something wrong in your body? Let's chase it away.

Feel the love energy pour through your crown chakra. Feel the washing of Spirit. Do not let these things encompass you with fear, for they are phantoms... waiting, waiting for your miracle. Know these things, as Kryon sits in front of your feet, ready to wash each one in Love.

And so it is.

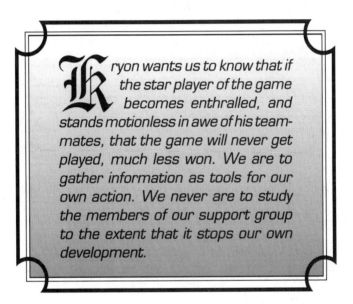

ryon wants us to know that if the star player of the game becomes enthralled, and stands motionless in awe of his teammates, that the game will never get played, much less won. We are to gather information as tools for our own action. We never are to study the members of our support group to the extent that it stops our own development.

Chapter Twelve

Science

Science

Chapter Twelve

From the writer...

There is so much about science that I wish to ask Kryon, but I already know that this is a subject that cannot be answered as clearly as I would like. The reason is a good one, and very understandable: if we are given answers on a platter (without working for them), then there is no learning, and no helping the planet through self-discovery. Kryon has told us repeatedly that the new science will come in the next years through being balanced and enlightened. Humans will help humans. This is as it should be, and I honor this process. Meanwhile I am bursting with curiosity anyway!

It doesn't hurt to ask the questions; even if Kryon will not answer directly, he often gives us hints and insights into the working of things. And who knows, perhaps the information that follows will actually be the catalyst to someone who will use the hints to put the first antigravity machine together! The Universe is laughing at this, since it indeed knows that I have good intuition as to the truth of this statement.

There is an underlying feeling to the Kryon work that as the channeler I feel constantly. It is this: everything is logical, and follows order. Even the most bizarre of events to us follow universal order and physics. Again I state that today's scientific understanding was yesterday's magic. If you truly see this, then you can understand how today's magic is tomorrow's understanding. Metaphysics will have to change its name when the philosophy is no longer "beyond-physics"... and this is a distinct possibility. Granted, the full workings of the Universe will not be ours to know as long as we are in "lesson," but much of the relationship between mind and matter that at this writing is so much "hocus pocus" to the scientist, will be defined and understood.

I can't imagine a better master entity to ask about science, for Kryon's work revolves around the magnetic. This means that he is working with the very essence of our Earth science's core, for magnetics is the basic "handshake" between our biology and the land. It is involved in the great mystery of gravity, and the debate of light nomenclature and sub-atomic particle behavior.

This writer preface is again written before the channeling, so that you can again join me in my thoughts prior to any answers regarding this subject. Let us see what Kryon has to say first...

Regarding science...

Science

Greetings Dear Ones. As your partner has stated, I will never give you information that will expose the duality, or raise questions for the Earth scientists to ponder that would risk the new levels of learning that you are in. However, I am permitted in the appropriateness of your new energy to give you hints that may appear for the first time in these readings. The reason for this is to prod the special ones who are reading this information, to use these hints to solve the science problems that are before them. This information, combined with the natural new energy that you have earned, will provide answers.

All through the writings and channelings so far, I have occasionally given you information that is of value toward the explanation of things you are now pondering. An example: although you may have quickly passed it, early on in this book I told you of a phenomenon that undoubtedly your science is seeing right now, but that may not be published. There are very high energy, short gamma ray bursts hitting your at-

mosphere. Do you remember why? Look back in these writings for the answer. It has a spiritual solution... which is not uncommon in your physics, for the spiritual is forever married to the physical. The spiritual is the basis for your science, and sets the rules for the observations that you see daily. *

The painter came one day and covered the Earth with love and spiritual attributes. This stained the land with energy, and the land responded with life and balance, forever unifying the painter with

*see page 228

the land and the life force on it. Humans, who were given the task to walk the Earth shielded from the reality of the truth, have been recently finding evidence of the paint. They continue, however, to disavow the existence of the painter, having found no reason to believe that the paint didn't create itself. When some day they finally acknowledge the painter, the balance of the three will be clear, and the attributes of the paint will no longer mystify them. Without the painter, there is no consciousness of why the colors were mixed as they were, or why they worked together at all.

Regarding Earth science in general, I give you an admonishment regarding your scientific method. It is backward from the way it should be! It is actually upside down, so to speak. You should be looking at all phenomena, no matter how bizarre they may seem to you, and be asking the question: is there consistent correlation within these phenomena that demand investigation? Instead you look at only what you know, then you extract assumptions that only fit what you understand (or think you understand). You apply the assumptions to the things you observe around you, and if your small postulates don't fit what is actually happening, you often discount what's happening entirely. Dear ones, this will not serve you. An example: with this method you have effectively discounted the natural dipole balance of the human body's organs; therefore, the way to measure it and balance it has been ignored, even though the evidence of this is all around you, and has been for centuries. How can you ignore something that is so obvious?

Also, you have discounted astrological influences, thereby denying that the solar system's motion interacts with your magnetics, both planetary and biological. How long will it take you to learn to work backward from the overall phenomena? You should be saying, "This phenomenon, no matter how odd, warrants investigation – because it is there, and it seems to be consistent. If there is correlation within its operation to something of Earth or human value, then what are the workings of it?" Instead you are saying: *"The things I have studied and understand work a certain way, and I have discovered the basics as to why. When I apply my understanding to large unexplained phenomena, it doesn't fit. Therefore I deny the existence or reality of the new phenomena. "* Do you see how this is backward? The larger *whole* should dictate the study of the *parts* that make it work. Instead you are examining individual parts, and extrapolating the assumed universal working of the whole!

Imagine that 50,000 years from now a culture far different from yours lands on Earth and uncovers a small part to one of your complex space launch vehicles. From this they extrapolate the probable use for the part, and the purpose of the vehicle. Then they project what the vehicle must have been like, based on understanding from science they have in their culture... and they write it into their history of humans, complete with drawings. Much later their children grow up, come back to Earth and discover the actual whole vehicle intact, but they don't recognize it. It is ten times the size they thought, and it's shaped all wrong to ever "fly." And it has no bearing whatsoever to the human vehicle they learned about in their history books, and saw drawings of. They classify the space behemoth, therefore, as some kind of Earth art, or space statue, that humans must have worshiped. After all, it couldn't have been useful based on the history they already "knew" about humans. Do you see how the "worship" of the part tainted the reality of the whole? If this culture had discovered the rocket first, then all might have been different.

In your case the "rocket" of this story is all around you, and you have the benefit of the workings of the whole every day. Unfortunately many of your Earth scientists and religious leaders have already created the "drawings" of their scholarly opinions of how the whole must work, but when they see the reality of the whole, they don't recognize it. It doesn't fit their postulated model, and they therefore discount that it could be what it actually is!

Scientists, listen: How do those from other cultures accomplish major human healing so often, in such mystifying ways? Does this warrant real investigation, or have you disavowed its existence, since it doesn't fit your model? How does the human body miraculously eliminate disease by itself almost overnight? There is consistent documentation of this, and it correlates to thought energy. What do you make of it? ... or are you ignoring it? There are also consistent correlations regarding magnetic attributes to human behavior and health. Look for them. Finally begin to understand about polarity and magnetism in the arena of health and behavior. This will serve you immensely, and will give you tools to increase your life span now! This is old technology. Rediscover it!

Also, put your ego to one side, and ask the serious astrologer about this discounted system in your culture. Let this person show you the strong correlations, and the enormous human history of its belief and use through thousands of years of human existence. Then attack the "hows and whys" scientifically from the outside in, for that is your specialty of investigation, logic and discovery. Build your own model of how it works scientifically! Then add it to your list of human tools, and use it for your benefit. Astrology is not mystical. It is science!

Why is it that you do not wish to investigate these seemingly intangible things? This is not an admonishment, but a real question, for there is indeed a reason why you do not seek these things. There is spiritual responsibility connected with these discoveries... and there lies an entirely different subject!

Remember this: the closer you get to the actual physical truth of things, the closer you will be to spiritual basics. If your belief system discounts the spiritual as having no part of science, then you will soon reach a personal impasse. When others around you, who have no such bias, begin to show progress and understanding in their scientific work, with working postulates and proven success, will you then discount them as well? You are quickly racing toward either a bridge or a wall. One is ignorance, and one is revelation. None of you have to suddenly become spiritual or "weird," to cross this bridge. All that is necessary is for a mind that is open to **all possibilities**, not just the ones you have felt should be acceptable.

I remain the mechanic, the magnetic master and the scientist. I remain in love,

Kryon

Chapter Thirteen

Questions about
Science

Questions about Science

Chapter Thirteen

Question: I want to start right out with the biggest question I have, and that many wish to know about. Can we discover antigravity? If such a thing exists, do UFOs use it?

Answer: Your term antigravity is a misnomer. You must completely change your concept of how this property may take place before you understand it. Would you tell a person that he is filled with anti-love if he were angry? Gravity is an absolute product of the attributes of mass & time, one of which you may change.

What I am about to describe to you is not new, but has not yet been developed on your planet. It has been observed here by humans, but because of timing, it was never allowed to be developed. No universal entity ever stopped it, but by "timing" I mean that the technology to expand and experiment with it was not ready... and therefore nothing happened when it was discovered.

Know this: your physics laws are mostly correct. You have done a fine job of observing and documenting the physics of the most common objects around you. Your mathematics are good, and the postulates you apply to the way mass behaves is also good; however, you make interesting but understandable assumptions about all mass. You already know that gravity is an attribute of mass, and is always there. What has been missing so far in your thoughts has been how gravity is related to time (something you cannot easily conceive of or change), and that the entire issue of gravity, mass and time is nonlinear.

Let us speak of just the mass/gravity issue. Within the far reaches of the Universe you feel that you have observed objects with great mass and gravity, but small physical size. This leads you to conclude that density is also very important in the mass formula. Your idea of how mass became dense, however, is not altogether accurate.

You have been able to measure how an object moves in space, and therefore guess its mass. If you also know its size, then you also can guess what it is made of... gas or rock, ice or vapor, etc., since you are computing density, your key to actual measured mass. Most of the Universe is made of elements that support simple size/density ratios, and the actual proof of a mystery object's mass and density is the way it moves in relation to other objects. It's when you find the objects that don't behave this certain way that you are mystified. Remember this: your observations are restricted to your own time frame. This means that since gravity properties are a result of mass and time – and I have also told you that they are non linear – you only really get to see the properties of your own time frame. If you were able to move from that position even slightly, you would see an entirely different scenario of gravity attributes.

Let's say that you, new to Earth, spent 30 years on a primitive island on the earth's Equator. Being a scientist using observation only, you studied the properties of water the best you could, until you felt that you totally understood it. It was all around you, more than you could ever imagine, and you were comfortable with its properties, everywhere you found it... the way it moved, the way it refracted visually, the way it flowed in smaller streams on land, and how much it weighed when transporting it. It became a physical certainty. Suddenly a spacecraft appears to whisk you to the North Pole, where in shock you discover a brand new attribute to water... it gets hard when it's very cold! Imagine... hard water: what a concept! You were never able to generate this condition, since your island could not simulate this. You thought you understood water, but you did not. This is much the same within your limited observation of mass on your own "time island."

Many of you have guessed correctly that magnetics and electricity play a critical part of the determination of the real attributes of mass, and that the magnetic variables that determine the mass product are often working within very small particles... to create the density of an object, and also its time frame!

Since you are able at a distance to see apparently small dense things with tremendous mass attributes (big mass / strong gravity), have you given any thought to the reverse? What I am telling you is that your so called "antigravity" is really your search for the mechanism to create the attributes of what I will call a "massless" condition. It is the small-particle mechanics which actually determine the mass attributes of an object, and therefore the gravity and time frame surrounding the object. Can you imagine an object with zero density, no matter what the size? Very little in the Universe exists in this condition, but it can be artificially created, simply using the density mechanics of what determines an object's actual mass.

Your science formulas really don't allow for this; even some of your best theories are not really ready for a massless object. Using your finest theories, you can extract that if what I am saying is correct, then the energy of a massless object would be zero. Since you have postulated that mass times the square of the speed of light equals the energy of an isolated system, your own postulate has to equal zero energy for a massless object. Can you imagine what situations an object with negative mass would create? What is your concept of negative energy? Also, although unrelated to this scientific discussion, you might be interested in the reaction of light to a massless object. You already have guessed that strong gravity will bend light. What do you think the total absence of mass, energy, and gravity does to light around an object? This is for you to ponder. While you are pondering it, also consider negative mass, negative energy, and gravity that is reversed!

Experimenting with a magnetic field's lines of influence running at right angles to another electric field will bring you gratification in your search to alter the mass of an object. These are the mechanics to actually temporarily change small particle polarity behavior... which translates to density, the lack of it, or its reverse (negative density). The amount, shape and other parameters of your work on this are up to you. As you discover how to alter these things, be cautious, for you will also be creating a small time displacement, which can be dangerous to you physically until you understand how objects in altered time displacements correctly interact.

Although you understand that such a mechanical system must be circular, do not make any assumptions about the shape of the interacting magnetic and electric fields, or what the medium should be to carry the polarity properties in such a system. Remember, however, that gas and liquid metals can also be used effectively to carry a charge. Although seemingly a mystery within the context of this discussion, do not be surprised if water under pressure also plays an important part in this system.

With great irony I tell you that this massless condition was accurately created in the primitive workshop of a great electrical scientist, in your culture on the American continent not too long ago. If you were able to visit his workshop, you would note the holes in the ceiling and the patched glass-covered light port where his massless objects literally took off and wildly flew everywhere. If he had been born 50 years later, he would have been able to control the attributes of his experiment. As it was, he did not have the precision tools you have now to direct and control such an experiment. It was his great passion to understand this phenomenon; but because it was so uncontrollable and sporadic, he was never able to bring others to see it work, for he could not accurately create it consistently. This depressed him greatly in his later years, for his was a great three-dimensional scientific mind... in a body which could not wait long enough for the tools to prove his creative ideas.

This massless condition is therefore not a new thought for you, and continues to be acknowledged as a viable property within many human groups; but still you have not been able to bring it to a working state. Perhaps this very channeling will prompt the one who is supposed to "discover" it... to get on with it!

Your question about the UFOs was insightful. This is part of the system they use to travel in your gravity. I have already given you clues as to what is actually going on within a massless object's influence, but understand that a true massless object no longer obeys the laws of your time frame physics. Wild starts and stops, speed and turns, are all well within the realm of a massless object, since it creates its own energy influence on that which is around it. Also be aware that as I have stated, the time reference of a massless object is slightly different from your own, making you appear to be slightly slower than the massless object. Its reaction to more traditional mass molecules around it is also predictable. Because of the very slight time displacement, it tends to change the number of electrons within the atoms directly in contact with it. This is a clue on how to detect a massless object, even if you cannot see it.

A true 100% massless object will be unaffected under the influence of your gravity field, and yet those machines which visit you have great maneuverability. This should tell you that mass attributes can be changed easily... and actually focused. What would happen if negative mass (out of synchronization with your time frame) was focused against your traditional mass? The answer is "repulsion." This is the result of a focusing of an artificial negative mass against the common mass of Earth. Therefore, you now have an indication that the attributes of mass are actually "tunable;" and with more than one "mass engine," a system of tied objects can be multi-faceted, or have multiple attributes at the same time. Certain sides of a tied system can be tuned to certain mass attributes, while the bottom, top, or other sides can be tuned differently... something that does not exist within the Universe in natural form. Not only can one attribute, or system-side, be negative mass (in a repulsion mode against common mass), but one side can also be common mass that is heavier than another side. Precision coordinated, this system can allow finely controlled movement in all planes. This should also now explain the magnetic anomalies around the UFO experiences that you have documented, and the "sounds" they make in your radio receptors. The sounds are not sounds at all, but just the result of constantly fine tuning the density of the mass engines, of which there can be as many as seven. The magnetics involved interfere with your radio transmissions, which are, after all, magnetic. Each mass engine controls a rather small focused mass plate. Quite often many vehicle's systems are "tied together" in one controlled system, so many craft appear to move exactly together as one. This is an efficient way of keeping the mass engines of many systems from interfering with each other as they react to your Earth gravity. It isn't just efficient;. it's necessary.

In order for this system to work, the operator of the engines must fully understand the common mass attributes of the objects that he is pushing and pulling against, for the laws of gravity remain constant within a given time frame, and only the mass density and polarity of the vehicle plates are changed to push or pull against a known mass quantity. Gravitational anomalies of Earth can create havoc with a system such as this, and this is why sometimes these vehicles crash. There are known and unknown anomalies of gravitational consistency on your planet. Believe me, most are now well mapped in the log books of those who visit here regularly. They are like the hidden rocks in a peaceful harbor... to a wooden Earth ocean ship.

Much of the technical advancement in this field will be to apply very high and low density attributes to smaller and smaller amounts of matter, thereby reducing the size of the apparatus doing the work. The more you learn about atomic structure, the more this will become clear, and it is the understanding of small particle polarity and behavior that is the key to all of this. Perhaps your quest should begin with the very small, learning how the atoms respond to each other given the exposure to specific electrical parameters. Even a very small distance change between nucleus and the orbit parts of the atoms can make a large difference in mass density. Find out what the "rules" are for why the distance is so great between the nucleus and the orbiting parts. How can you change it?

A final admonition to all of this, and one of great importance. Protect yourself while you experiment! The results of just one efficient mass engine can damage your biology with very little exposure! When you finally discover how to use the system, you will have to protect yourselves if you decide to travel within the system. Shielding is necessary! Experiment with crushed crystal as an insulator as a start. You will quickly discover the properties of this, and the rest will be obvious.

Question: I'm glad I asked! Speaking of atomic structure, is there anything startlingly new yet to discover that we have not found yet?

Answer: Yes. Besides the above discussion of what happens to matter when you start manipulating polarities, there will be new parts to discover as well. One of the most interesting things, however, will be when you discover the "twins."

Hiding within common atomic structure is a marvelous peek at something that will totally and completely mystify you, for it will seem to break all the laws of time and space. The "twins" are a pair of atomic parts that always relate to each other, and are always found in pairs. I will not tell you where to look. Believe me, you will know when you have found them. A few already have seen their "footprint."

Their behavior will astound you. You will discover that when stimulated correctly, they will always move together as a pair. When you start separating them by distance to experiment, they will continue to move exactly together. No matter how far you remove them from one another, they will exactly move together. Even if one is launched into space to travel beyond your solar system, they will still move as one. If one is stimulated, the other will move. They are forever a pair, and are indestructible. If one's energy is converted, then the other will do the same.

This will cause you to totally reexamine your ideas of time and space, for this condition will not follow the "ultimate speed" of transmission that you thought was correct, that of the speed of light. You will have discovered something that travels faster than you can ever measure! This instant communication between the parts of the "twins" is the basis of communication of all universal Spirit entities in the Universe. It is the mechanism in 1987 that let all instantly know of Earth's readiness for a change. It is how I instantly communicate with the great creative force, and it conforms to the shape of the Universe... which I gave you in earlier channelings.

Question: Can we, in lesson, ever truly understand the real shape of the Universe?

Answer: No. This would not be appropriate, and at the same time keep you in lesson. Your duality would be revealed, and this would not serve the situation of what you are successfully accomplishing on the planet. Some day when the Earth is no longer in lesson as you know it, much more will be known by humans here.

Question: I am interested in computers. Where is this technology going? Are we on the right path to creating machines that will help us? Are computers dangerous?

Answer: Your computing technology was absolutely necessary to allow you to proceed with the new-age science. Look at the leaps of endeavor you were allowed. Whenever you see this kind of scientific acceleration, you should know that it is appropriate. What you do with the knowledge, however, is your test of lesson. Will it always be used for a weapon? ... or now will it be used for the environment and good health discoveries for the many?

In regard to computer technology, you are missing the most obvious thing imaginable! When you see the Earth's most amazing computer operating in biological beings all around you, why haven't you emulated it? Do you wish to always have half a technology, or do you want the full technology?

You will increase your computer science instantly by 10,000-fold if you will start combining what you already know with chemistry. The electrochemical computing machine is the way of the Universe. It is the way of your own biology, and of your own brain. When will you start investigating merging the two together?

This has nothing whatsoever to do with the creation of living cells. It is simply a technology that combines electrical parameters with chemical ones, to create undreamed of power and speed... much like you have now in your own heads. How would you like a computer that remembers everything that has happened within it for 50 years, stored in the space of a walnut? Many technical science answers can be obtained from an emulation of what has already been done by Spirit within your Earth nature.

Question: In previous writings you said that our nuclear waste was one of the biggest dangers we currently have. The stuff seems indestructible, and it is volatile forever! What can we do about it?

Answer: Your active atomic waste is indeed the largest danger you face. You have already seen how a vast portion of land can be poisoned for lifetimes simply by one atomic accident. Think of the tragedy of losing part of your country to such a condition... simply by ignoring items buried deep underground that are building to a critical point in their activity. Right now as you read this, you have a small city on your own American continent, whose name begins with "H," that is prime for this condition. Disaster will indeed happen if you ignore it, since it is simple basic physics. You don't have to wait for catastrophe before acting, however.

Do not entertain the idea of throwing the waste away, for this is unnecessary and most often will not work. An active substance such as this is like acid. Whatever you do with it will only be temporary, until it eats out of whatever you place it into. Never, ever put it into your oceans or lakes!

The real answer should be obvious. It must be neutralized. I spoke of this in earlier channelings, but now I will expand on it. There are many ways of neutralizing this waste, but the one which is currently within your technology is simple and available now. You should immediately turn to Earth biology! Look for the micro organisms you already know about that can devour these active substances, and make them harmless. Develop them using your science to increase their number and efficiency, and let them eat your waste!

You might ask why this is not being done now, since these organisms have already been discovered. Look to your world governments for the answers. Demand that the research be complete, and that the process begin! Understand the Earth politics of why this has not been exposed fully to you, or funded properly. An organism of this sort is small, easy to transport and grow, and doesn't care if it feeds on a weapon or a waste dump.

It's time for the Earth leaders to put away fear of technologies that might change the weapon balance. It is the irony of science that quite often new discoveries can be used for peace or war, and it is your enlightenment that determines which. Right now you are poised on some of the finest environmental tools ever developed... including the one I speak of to reduce your nuclear waste. You are also prime to receive a great deal of technology useful to increase your life spans, enhance disease control, and affect your health in general. Do not let the fear in the few hold back the good for the many.

Question: Kryon, I suspect that being human, I can't understand your constant reference to the fact that we are on "linear time," and that the Universe is on "now" time. Is there any kind of example you can give to further clarify this? It's really confusing how the two can exist simultaneously.

Answer: Your intuition serves you well, for you cannot truly understand how this works until you are no longer a part of it. This is the essence of your duality, and it is appropriate for it to remain shielded. I will, however, give you a very simple and brief analogy regarding what you wish to know. Imagine a train track that is constructed in a very large circle. There is a small train on it that represents you. It is always in motion, traveling approximately the same speed. The track is your linear time frame and the train is you, in linear time motion, always moving forward from where you were to where you will be.

The universal entities, including the Kryon, stand toward the center of the circle watching you traverse your linear time. Since the Universe built the track, and the tracks around it of other linear time events, it knows exactly where it is going, and what events will eventually come along to break your circle. That is, we know how long your sun will last, and when the various appointments are with colliding bodies. All this is very, very far away in your linear time. We therefore are standing still, watching you in motion. At any time we wish, we can look to the left or right, observing not only what was, but the place where your train will be in the future. This is how we can be in the static "now" while you are in motion.

What we do not know, however, is what you are going to do with your train on the track we have built. How many cars will you add or subtract; what color will the train be? Will you destroy the train? Will you clean it up and repair it, or let it go into disrepair until it stops? Will you make it more efficient, thereby changing its speed? All these things are open to you.

This is the scenario, and it is why we can say to you that although there is no predestination of your personal future from the Universe, we still know where all the tracks lead to.

Question: There is beginning to be a great deal of scientific and religious objection to the new-age teachings. When I read these critical publications, some of them make sense to me, with valid arguments regarding the premise that "if it's there, and it's real, then why can't we see it, touch it, measure it, and get it to repeat itself?" Your statements early on about everything from gravity, astrology, and healing are under fire from these men and women, many of whom are very smart, open minded and willing to listen to reason. What do you say to this?

Answer: In the early 1700s a fine, smart, God-fearing man stands on the eastern coast of your continent, wearing the garb of a pilgrim. He is full of honor and respect for nature and God. He is there by design, having chosen the difficult path to break from those others whom he felt had compromised their integrity in divine matters. His intent, therefore, was seen by all (including Spirit) as genuine. He successfully led his people to a new beginning in a new land.

Along the way he is sought out by another man who sees the pilgrim as close to God. This other man confides a vision he has had: he claims to have seen the future. This man tells the pilgrim that there are invisible waves in the air that are able to carry a voice to great distances. He says that it will be possible someday to speak to someone in the mother continent instantly... and his vision goes on to speak of even music and other wonders traveling in the air. The pilgrim knows this is nonsense, since he has had no vision of this himself (being close to God), and the science of the day has never seen any evidence whatsoever of it.

Disgusted by this "insane" man, the pilgrim calls on God to strike him down, feeling that his very essence is evil. The man is led away and later killed because he was considered in league with the Devil.

Not much has changed in this scenario within your modern day. The sophistication of your society has tempered it, but the essence of what happened in the 1700's example is still there. Your religious leaders are calling the Kryon the work of the devil, and your scientists are telling you that they have no evidence whatsoever of the validity of your writings; therefore you have no credibility. To them you are a clown, and to the religious leaders you are satanic

Go back for a moment to the pilgrim. The man with the vision, of course, was correct. Radio waves are magnetic, and were all around the pilgrim, even as he stood there denying them... since the Universe creates them naturally. The waves were in existence waiting to be discovered and utilized to carry voice and music. The pilgrim couldn't see them; and in addition, his science had absolutely no way to measure them yet. Therefore, the waves didn't exist to him. Added to this was the fact that anyone seeing the future who was not authorized to do so by the church, and the accepted writings of the church, were seen to be satanic.

It's only a matter of time before these teachings are very real to you, and exist for your science. Unlike the hundreds of years it took for you to discover the invisible waves from the time of the pilgrim, you will discover some of the invisible truths of the Kryon within decades from now instead of centuries... And so I say to these who doubt: ***be careful how you judge the messenger, just because of your ignorance of the message***.

Question: Finally a medical question: will we ever conquer AIDS?

Answer: You must know by now that I cannot give you your future. It isn't because I am restrained, but because you control it completely! I will enjoy the surprises as much as you. What I can tell you is that the mechanism for its control is well within your grasp. With the kind of enlightened progress your planet has shown recently, Spirit is expecting that you will find it, and with it much more regarding the mechanics of small particle biology invasion. Although cryptic to many, my former channelings on small biology particle mechanics contain answers. It is indeed possible that by the time these writings are released, the answers to your question will already be at hand. Remember: polarization and magnetics play a far more important part in your health than you currently give credit for. There is much to discover!

Kryon *... in the News*

Predictions of scientific observation of the incoming guides & masters!

See page 67, Channeled Aug 1993
See page 208, Channeled Dec 1993

Gamma-ray bursts: A distant stretch?

Like firecrackers exploding in the night sky, gamma-ray bursts unleash a torrent of high-energy photons before fizzling out hundredths to tens of seconds later. These flashes of radiation rank among the most mysterious phenomena in the universe: No one has found the sources of the bursts, and it's uncertain whether the flashes originate within our galaxy or far beyond.

SCIENCE NEWS, VOL 14
FEBRUARY 5 1994

Scientists listen carefully to odd bursts in the sky

WASHINGTON - Mysterious double bursts of radio emissions, originating near the surface of the Earth, have been detected by a small satellite designed to spot nuclear blasts... Since the first sighting Nov. 5, an instrument known as Blackbeard - mounted aboard the Los Alamos National Laboratory's $17 million ALEXIS satellite - has recorded about 100 of the bursts, "the likes of which have never been described in scientific literature," said Dan Holden, Blackbeard's principal investigator.

THE GRAND RAPIDS PRESS
FEBRUARY 15 1994

Chapter Fourteen

Final Questions

Final Questions

Chapter Fourteen

From the writer:

The following are questions that simply did not seem to fit into any category of their own.

Question: Kryon, if you were invited to appear before the American president (currently President Clinton), what would be the prime directive of your comments?

Answer: This answer may surprise you. Although I have spoken about nuclear waste, magnetic Earth issues, and environmental admonitions, the strongest communications so far have been about your self-discovery as individuals and as a planet.

We believe in your duality struggle! Have you ever asked me what Spirit believes will happen on Earth? ... This is a question within these pages that I have now asked for you! Spirit (and the Kryon) believe that you will survive, grow, and elevate yourselves far beyond what was originally expected. This is why there is so much activity around you now. This is why we send our finest and strongest entities to assist you in all appropriateness. This is why we love you so! This is why I am here.

You are _really_ doing the work! You are succeeding... and we honor you greatly for your struggle for truth within the limitations of your duality. We believe you are headed for great discovery, peace between nations, and individual self-discovery in the process. This all may seem slow to you, but it will be accelerated as your time goes on.

If I could ask anything of your American government, as well as the other leaders of your planet, I would ask for their help in letting you see some universal truth, by letting go of the information they hold regarding the 50-year documented history regarding visitors you have had from off planet.

Old energy world government was about control. New energy government will eventually be about organization and coordination for environment, health and peace. Secrets of the nature I have spoken of will no longer serve the planet, for it is time for you to understand the scope of your place in the universal community. With this knowledge will come many questions regarding your future, your science and your religion. It will create the catalyst that you are lacking now to bring you together as a world... and in the process you will receive great self-discovery, for it will affect each individual personally. You cannot have this information without pondering your place within it.

I would ask your President to allow for a full disclosure of all that is known on the subject of real UFOs that has been documented, both for himself and for you, since even he does not know the complete story. I would tell him that he and his nation are ready for the truth, and can handle it, even the negative parts. Release all communications and images. Tell the complete story, even the embarrassing parts. I would also tell him that if he does not do this, it may happen anyway by itself within the next 20 Earth years when communication to the population happens directly; and it will be an angry public that finds out that in the face of such historic consequence, a few had the truth for three fourths of a century... and decided to keep it a secret.

You have earned the right to know of your place in the cosmos within the appropriateness of lesson. You will be far more prepared to deal with the different kinds of visitors if you are given advance notice of their existence. Otherwise mistakes may be made in fear and ignorance that might delay your enlightenment and cosmic understanding for years.

Also, the obvious... if you finally have the truth about the visitors, the inappropriate ones will be less likely to visit freely, and the appropriate ones may even give you science information! Count on it! Some day when this book is discovered in the ancient archives of your libraries, you will laugh at the apparent naivete of this revelation, just as you now muse at those in your own history who feared to sail off the edge of the Earth when they were searching for other life on the planet.

Question: I never thought of letting you ask your own questions! Tell me something else you wish us to know... even without me asking it.

Answer: A very wise question, one of the finest of the lot. After all, how can you ask about revelations you don't know about?

A very exciting phenomenon walks the Earth with you at this moment. It is present in the "new seed." There is a group of young people, whose number I will not reveal, that carry a charged potential DNA change for the human race!

I previously channeled to you that in 1987 your planet was interrogated. At that time it was decided that, much to the delight and surprise of many in the Universe, your planet of free choice was found to contain the quality of energy frequency that would allow it to continue into the next phase... that being of graduation! There was much celebration over this fact, and it is the precise reason why I am here now, to facilitate the grid adjustments to allow you more enlightenment. Part of the equation is that not only are you allowed implants to void karma and move on into a new energy perspective, but you also are given the gift of an evolvement in biology.

In the years 1978 to 1982 there were a group of humans born that were indeed special, for they carried the charged potential of your DNA change. It was projected that their age would correspond to the 1987 interrogation, and if your Earth was found not to be ready, they would be terminated. As you know, this was not the case, so they remain walking among you. Who are they? Shamans of the Earth will recognize them instantly, for they carry attributes of this status, since they are the "new breed."

When I say that they carry the charged potential of your evolvement, I mean this: alone they can do nothing for the planet. They must procreate. It is in this process that the catalyst of their potential will be released. The offspring of the union with normal humans will bring about a subtle but observable change in your DNA. If they should happen to procreate with each other, nothing unusual will take place; it is only with normal humans that the potential will be realized.

Here are the admonitions involved with these: I speak of these admonitions since there are those reading this now that have control over such things, and vibrate in total harmony to what I am exposing.

1. Hide these individuals carefully! They are in danger from those who believe they threaten the doctrinal religion of Earth. Those who believe they have the "truth," to the total exclusion of all other humans, are the ones who ironically will endeavor to destroy the real destiny of the planet.

2. Do not keep these individuals celibate! It is in procreation that the entire purpose of Spirit will be fulfilled. It will be tempting

to enlist them in the Earth's protective religions, and hide them to the exclusion of their real purpose.

3. Do not worship them. Not only is it not appropriate, but it will call attention to who they are, and place them in real danger.

What the Kryon really wants you to know: I have asked my partner to close this second book with my recurring message of love for you.

Do you ever find yourself longing for that loving parent to hold you in its arms, and look down on you in unconditional love? Perhaps you are tired of your life here, weary of walking through your karmic lessons. You long for the love and feeling of something you barely remember? Dear ones, your ineptness is a result of the separation from God. In this case God is your own higher self! It perhaps seems to be oversimplified that all of your despair or Earthly problems could lie at the feet of something so basic. Believe me when I tell you that it is indeed so.

There is a paper-thin layer that separates you from the love of Spirit. It is presented to you in all of these writings for your examination, your logical intellect, and your intuitive senses. All in all, it lies there dripping with potential, and even in some cosmic humor... for it smiles at you in the simplicity of its own process, and the difficulty of yours. Like a fortress door, many layers thick, with warning signs posted, it is a phantom joke, for it is the path to your enlightenment, and it remains unlocked at all times!

The arms of Spirit are huge. They are everything you remember and long for. As I seat myself figuratively before your feet in session, I see your potential, and my Spirit heart cries for you to find the truth of your process. For this new energy I adjust for you contains the sparks of joy, peace, physical healing and the very hope of the Universe! Those of you who turn your back on this are loved every bit as much as those who accept it. But there is so much more joy of Spirit celebrating those who choose to look in the face of something so difficult, only to suddenly find a familiar face looking back, the one they have known forever... a familiar remembered face that smiles in congratulations for a job well done. Then the arms of Spirit are free to support you in full enlightenment for the rest of your days in lesson.

Why would you ever choose to be without this great gift?

I indeed love you dearly... as Spirit itself!

Chapter Fifteen

Writer Notes

Writer Notes

Chapter Fifteen

From the writer:

Well ... I gave myself my own chapter! It's not that what I have to say is so important, but that this information also deals with questions and answers regarding the Kryon story.

The Reality

The great cosmic joke around my life is that I'm so hard to "reach." I spent a great deal of my life scoffing at people doing exactly what I am now doing! In addition, I have always been one not to believe anything whatsoever unless I really felt there was fact behind it... and here I am channeling.

You might ask (others have): what does it take for a person such as myself to come to this point? channeling an off-Earth entity from beyond? Some feel that I have indeed "lost it," and I am in some kind of reality haze. *"With his feet planted firmly in the air, he has struck the nail squarely on the thumb!"* ... I can hear them saying.

The cosmic humor in all this is that Spirit chose someone who not only was incredibly skeptical, but remains so! As I have written before, I was dragged kicking and complaining to two separate psychics three years apart... and had them spell Kryon's name in session, and tell me he wanted to "get through" to me. Only when I surrendered to logic did I finally start to channel the information.

...ONLY WHEN I SURRENDERED TO LOGIC??

That's just the point here. Spirit (God) has shown me over and over that we are supposed to use our logical brains, as well as our intuition. Over and over in this book Kryon has told us that our reality changes as we discover new facts and ideas, and that tomorrow's commonplace is today's magic. I believe this now, and I finally realize what this message actually means. It means that **it is illogical to base our belief (or unbelief) for any subject. on a static reality**. Do you want to know the next evolutionary step in man's thinking? Tolerance in personal decision making... weighing the difference between what is seen (and therefore felt as real), and the logical certainty of future discovery and informational change.

Kryon has said repeatedly (and I paraphrase): **Scientists**, what will you do when the "little green men" land on the White House lawn and complain that your leaders were fools not to tell you about them? Will your eyes stop rolling when people speak of flying saucers? Will you change your idea of reality? ... or deny it in the face of fact? When you find the speed of light is only a perceived barrier, and that matter and time are related so strongly that they ignore the barrier as a general rule, will you remember you read it here? The admonishment: let your logic for the certainty of change, and the possibility of these alternate realities, open your mind to expanded thinking. It is illogical for you to do otherwise. If you don't, then you haven't changed your thinking in 400 years... you only have more blinking lights on your tools.

Kryon has said repeatedly (and again I paraphrase): **Religious leaders**, are you really interested in God? ... or only in what you have been taught God is? Could you be open for a change in facts? When the scrolls are finally examined and understood by non-biased scholars, will you accept the fact that you had bad information? Or will you call it the work of the Devil and continue on as before? The admonishment: let the Holy Spirit (Spirit) give you the truth! Stand away from what you thought you knew, and let God give you more understanding, and new realities about the mechanics of Spirit. Are you afraid of losing face... or just church members? The love remains!

I would not be writing books as these unless the experience was very real. How can I tell you what I see and hear except within the pages of a book such as this? I am pragmatic. What you cannot do is follow me around all day to watch my dialogue with Spirit. Everything that I have channeled, I claim as truth in my daily life. If Spirit says we should be able to have peace and tolerance over the barbs we experience daily that drive us nuts, then I expect that kind of a change in my life. (Isn't that logical?) If Spirit channeled that I can co-create my own reality, then I expect that too. If Spirit says I can stop aging so fast, I expect that!

The result personally is that I absolutely must live within the integrity of the channeled information. It never stops amazing me. I told Spirit early on: "*If you are going to put me through this, it better be real! ... I will not become a clown for a false entity, or alienate former church friends and close family, unless I see the truth exemplified around me both in my personal life and in the Kryon readers (like you), and light group members.*"

If you have been paying attention throughout the book, you already know about the readers' results: letters from all over claiming life-changing power.... many healings... and a great deal of self-awareness. Spirit is smiling now, and saying to me, "Is this proof enough? Does this satisfy your logic?" Spirit picked me because it knew that my attributes were difficult. It wanted the skeptical person reading this to relate to me a bit, maybe even to change a bit because of it.

As far as my personal life goes, I took the implant (of course), and it immediately changed my life. My reactions to others, my former karma, and the things that used to drive me nuts... all changed. Everyone noticed it, even the guys at work. I wasn't satisfied, however, and I wanted more. I gave intent to let Spirit take me to the limit of my contract, and that's when things really turned upside down (don't do this unless you mean it).

This book is entitled "Don't Think Like a Human," not just because one of the live channeling sessions dealt with that, but mainly because that channeling was for me! It is my main flaw, and it needed to be exposed. The same month I gave intent, my 23-year-old business was shaken to the core by events around it beyond my control. The problem seemed to have no resolution, and the future of my entire career *appeared* bleak. All those around me told me that there was no solution. I was indeed that individual in the Kryon session, on the road, speeding toward the chasm without a bridge (p137). My biology screamed at me to worry and put on the brakes... but the love of Spirit sat on my shoulder and said, *"You don't know what we know. Trust us; keep pouring on the coal. Can you go any faster?"* The result was that I had to use the very co-creative steps that Kryon gave us in channeling. This was so that I could tell people what to expect, what it felt like, and how Spirit worked it out. The resolution was truly miraculous, almost like moving a mountain! It worked! That was the day when I truly realized that the truth of Spirit had come down to visit me in a tangible "touch and feel" way. I was never the same.

Sometimes folks ask me: "Do you ever channel for yourself?" The answer is yes, but not in the same way I channel for others. This is where I received the wonderful words for the first time, "Spirit will never give you a snake when you ask for an apple." When I sat in my living room at 1:30am shortly after I realized that my contract was the apparent chaos around my business (by expressing intent), I received that exact message. This is when I really got to feel the love and the overview of the power of my "piece of God." In addition, I was told, "We will not forsake you..." over and over. I was in a very special place for a long time that night.

So I find myself in the process of living what I have channeled. In the process I have peace. In the process I have *logical faith*. Spirit says to me, "How many times do you have to see this work before it becomes your reality?" This is when we can have *logical faith*. The very word "faith" for me used to mean "trust in the unseen." Now it means "trust in the seen, because I see it work over and over." The first step is to test it; that's the most difficult one for me.

Speak to me of reality? This is the most real thing I have ever experienced.

Authorship

I want to make it clear to everyone why my photo is not in Book One, or this book either... and why my name isn't on the spine. Early on, I realized that the inclusion of my photo would tend to lead people to look at me instead of Kryon, and associate the words with my picture instead of Spirit. It's also so disappointing to see a photo at the end of any book that doesn't look at all like you expected. (The fact that I have two noses, and my ear is on my forehead doesn't influence my decision at all.)

The reason my name isn't on the spine is similar. I'm not the author, but the writer. The author's name is on the spine. You should see what I went through with the distributors regarding this. For some reason they only want to list humans in their author listings... a strange thing. It's for this reason that my name had to go on the back cover.

By the time Book Three is released, I will have been around giving enough book signings and workshops that my face will no longer be a mystery... so maybe I'll put it in then. Unless I get letters asking me not to... which is a distinct possibility when they see what I look like.

Appendix A

The Temple of Rejuvenation

Appendix A

From the writer...

Within the live channelings in Chapter Eleven of this book, Kryon referenced the Temple of Rejuvenation two times, and took us there during "journeys" (pages 107 and 153). Architect Mark Wonner, present during many sessions, illustrated the temple which appears on page 160. This is his question statement to Kryon regarding the specifics of the Temple, and Kryon's answers.

Mark: Greetings, Kryon Group. The following questions are intended to seek clarity and direction about the design of the
Temple of Rejuvenation in ways that may affect the illustration
to be included in the second book. In addition to these questions are inquiries that move beyond the present mission. We
now wish to continue the dialogue about this project so that it
may move along its destiny path.

Kryon: Greetings, Dear One! Your work and time spent for Spirit in
this endeavor is honored indeed. It is no accident that you find
yourself identifying so strongly with this structure. Do you remember yet? Much of an ancient past childhood was spent in the
company of your father, who cared for a structure much like this
one. It is very familiar to you. The karma you carry around it is
in the form of unfulfillment, or the feeling of same, for you did
not reach an appropriate age where you could actually participate in the ceremony, or be the target of its wonderful science.
It seems that the Earth had an agenda of its own that precluded
your continuance. Many surround you who were also terminated
at this time, and they too have this "seed fear" of coming close
to something they remember so well. Again, we thank you for
your efforts, for although it will cause you some anxiety to walk
into the middle of its remembrance, it will also have the effect of
canceling your fear, to really expose who you are. Your work will
bring about action in your life, and your intent will be rewarded
in many ways.

As my partner told you, I will not answer all of your questions, for it would expose certain attributes of the Temple that must be discovered through experimentation and enlightened endeavor. Here, however, are the answers I can give: Within the very short ones are great wisdom.

The Inner Chamber:

Mark: Starting from the core of the Temple and working our way out, present understandings of the Inner Chamber are thus:

The Chamber is a sphere that is divided into two equal hemispheres at the horizontal plane. The floor of the Chamber is mounted on, and supported by, the lower hemisphere. Within the Chamber are two tables. One table is located on the floor and is centered on the vertical axis of the chamber sphere. This table receives the target human. The table rotates about the vertical axis under the direction of the one who stands before the Control Table. The Control Table is located on the floor of the Chamber and off axis. The Control Table is under the direction of one whom you have termed the Priest of The Day." The Day Priest is assisted by several others who gather around the table. On the Control Table are two small spheres located near to the edge. These objects assist the Priest of The Day to adjust the Temple to the needs of the target human. The Control Table is a circle. The target table is attended by one of the assistants who cares for the needs of the one who reclines upon it.

1. **M**. Can you clarify any possible misunderstandings in the above statement?
    K. The center "target" turntable is not centered on the room. Its axis is approximately 3 meters from the room's axis.

2. **M**. Does the Control Table rotate?
    K. No.

3. **M**. Is the Control Table mounted on a pivoting platform that is flush or raised a step above the floor?

K. The control table is fixed permanently and slightly elevated. It is built so that the Day Priest always faces the axis of the room.

4. **M**. Is the target table mounted on a pivoting platform that is flush or raised a step above the floor?
    K. The target table is on a turntable. It is raised naturally by part of a device that will remain unrevealed at this time, but that will, during ceremony, lift this table to a mid point between floor and ceiling.

5. **M**. What is the distance in meters or feet from the axis of the Chamber to the Control Table?
6. **M**. What is the inside diameter of the Chamber of Rejuvenation sphere?
7. **M**. What is the outside diameter of the Chamber sphere?
    K.   No actual interior or exterior dimensions are appropriate to give. This will reveal too much about the size of the magnetic structure within.

8. **M**. Does the entire floor of the Chamber pivot?
9. **M**. Does any diameter of the floor pivot?
    K. Yes! The entire picture is thus: The entire floor of the chamber is a turntable. The control table is fixed or mounted toward the outer perimeter, always with the Priest facing the center axis of the room. The target table is on a separate turntable/lift that rotates independently at different directions and velocities than the overall floor. If you can imagine this in motion, you will see how the magnetic action in the direct center of the room will be able to "touch" or spill onto every part of the complex moving target table, as opposed to a focus of energy on a single spot.

10. **M**. Does the upper hemisphere pivot about the vertical axis at the floor or does the upper sphere pivot some distance above the floor level?
    K. The upper hemisphere is static, and does not move. Your perception is a remembrance of something else within the room pivoting which is high up.

11. **M**. Does the lower hemisphere move?
    K. The lower hemisphere is static, and does not move.

12. **M**. Is there access to the lower sphere? And if so, please describe what is contained therein, and why, and how is it accessed?
    K. Access to the lower sphere and the upper sphere are via lifts located in the outer "vestibule" perimeter area. These are not "service areas" as you might expect, but often-visited areas of control and alignment. Do not be surprised if there are technicians in these areas, appropriately shielded, during operation.

13. **M**. Is the Chamber floor supported by a structural ring at the perimeter, leaving the upper and lower hemispheres free to move about this fixed plane?
    K. No.

The Superstructure

Mark: We see the Inner Chamber Sphere contained within and supported by a structural shell building comprised of a ring of rooms and a perimeter corridor at the level of the Chamber floor. The ring corridor circulates persons involved with the activities of the Temple to and from Chamber and service spaces around it and to the five legs of the Temple which contain vertical circulation lifts, mechanical supply and return plenums and main structural support for the Temple of Rejuvenation Superstructure. The legs are of sufficient height to allow the lower spire to clear the base of the Temple. The understanding so far about this superstructure is that, in addition to its functional service to the Inner Chamber, the design of the outer form or skin of the superstructure is given over to the discretion and wisdom of the designers.

1. **M**. Does the form of the Temple Superstructure affect the performance characteristics of the Chamber in any way other than the materials used and the color of the exterior sheathing?

K. No. It is mainly aesthetic and ceremonial for the human to hold as sacred. This is appropriate, however, since it adds to honor for the ritual, thereby keeping the process the same for a very long time.

2. *M*. Are there any forms or materials that could be used on or as a part of the Superstructure that would enhance the functions of the Chamber?
    K. The main material used throughout this structure is that of crushed crystal. This exotic material is used almost solely for the purpose of human shielding. It has many forms within the building materials, and is used in odd ways. The process that produces it brings its color to a dull black.

3. *M*. Is there an ideal outer diameter of the main body of the Superstructure surrounding the Chamber?
    K. Yes.

The Spires

Mark: There are two spires. One is mounted upright with its circular base on or above the upper chamber hemisphere. The other is suspended under the lower Chamber with its circular base mounted to the lower hemisphere with the vertex pointing to the center of Earth. Both spires are in the form of perfect cones. Both are conical spires and are aligned with vertical axis of the Inner Chamber. Both spires have in them or on them at least one spiral.

1. *M*. On the preliminary sketch the angle of the spires is shown as 72 degrees above the horizontal plane. Is this good?
    K. 72 degrees is exactly accurate. Do you think you guessed this?

2. *M*. Do the spires need to actually touch the chamber sphere or should they be affixed to and supported by the superstructure?
    K. They are affixed and supported.

3. *M*. If they are attached to the superstructure, do the outer edges tangentially align with the chamber sphere? If not, describe their alignment.

K. Yes, they tangentially align. You have seen much of this very clearly, since it has a strong remembrance from a window of a room you were often kept in, that was close to where the bottom spire attached to the middle chamber.

4. *M*. The spires in the preliminary sketch have stepped spirals similar to the spiral ramp of the Minaret of the Great Mosque of al-Mutawakkil, Samarra, Iraq. The spiral may need to take another form however. I am not certain about this at this time. Is this a good way to design them? Should they be applied to the surface of the spire, or suspended away from the surface, or embossed into the surface, or flush with the surface?
    K. The initial sketch is more accurate than you know. It is indeed a continuous ramp in the approximate scale as drawn, and you have also given the correct number of 7. The spires are cast as one piece.

5. *M*. At times I have seen the spirals change their geometric progression from a constant gradient spiral to one that wants to accelerate/decelerate similar to a Fibunacci series spiral. Anything here?
    K. Go to questions 10 and 11

6. *M*. Can you inform us on the purpose of the spirals at this time?
    K. They are entirely ceremonial, and non scientific. They are simply a sheath for the temple's engines, but carry very specific meaning in their design, much like the pyramids do in your ancient desert continent. It is the engines within the spires that do the technical work, and this is where the new/ancient science is.

7. *M*. Is there more than one spiral per spire?
    K. One.

8. *M*. Are there counter spirals as in the dome of the Chapel of Anet?
    K. No.

9. *M*. Are there spirals shown in the preliminary sketch going in the correct direction?

K. It depends on which hemisphere of the Earth you are building in. One direction above the equator, another below. Do you remember the channeling on spinning? (Kryon enjoys making you search for answers.) The spirals are identically cast, however, for the area of the Earth, and are absolutely identical and interchangeable within the same structure.

10. *M*. I have seen in my mind's eye the spiral taking the form of a serpent/snake coiled around the conical upper spire. Is this ancient and auspicious symbol as seen on the Temple to be shown in the design or is this image for my own "amusement," so to speak? Please give any insight that is possible.

11. *M*. On occasion I have seen the upper spire altered from the pure form. Sometimes the vertex appears to be a gold "capstone" that is sometimes imbedded with crystals. Sometimes I see that the vertex is truncated at an angle or flat with a large flame or vertical beam of white light. Anything here?

    K. Your higher self is having fun. You have already "seen" the crystals within the exotic smooth surface, and you also get a glimpse of the true majesty of the science within, and the sacredness of the results. It was common to represent this temple in drawings as having a shaft of light connecting its top spire to the heavens. This was symbolic of the connection to the highest spirit power, and you have remembered it. As for the snake, it is the symbol of fear, warning that if you get to close to it, it will bite you again! Your seed fear raising its head again.

12. *M*. Are the spires hollow? If not, please describe for us what is in them and for what purpose.

    K. Yes, see question 6.

The Base

Mark: I have seen the Temple of Rejuvenation standing upon a terraced earthen and masonry pyramidal structure that is two or three stories high and very wide with access ramps, gardens, pools, waterfalls and the like. Contained within the base are facilities in service to the Temple such as assembly rooms, rest rooms, food service, meditation rooms, mechanical plants, maintenance shops, offices etc. Incorporated into the base structure are the foundations of the Temple legs and the access points to elevators within the legs.

1. **M**. Is there anything in this picture that may conflict with the purpose of the Temple?
    K. All as stated is correct, except that there is no amusement or food anywhere near the facility. All is sacred and practical. Emphasis on beauty is everywhere, and nature is honored.

2. **M**. Is the shape/form of the base in plan, elevation or section important to the function of the Temple? If so, please give what you can about this.
    K. The shape of the base is important for its support function and use. As you already know, it must support the structure, lift the bottom spire off the ground, and also allow for the mechanized lifts that the humans use to enter and exit as described in previous sessions. The angles and shape as drawn in your sketch are generally correct. Other aspect ratios will also work, and many temples differed in the base design, since this was not critical to the mechanism within. Functionality of support and use are the primary factors here, and nothing more. There were contests within those who built these temples for the most beautiful design, so there were variations.

3. **M**. Since ritual and ceremony are integral to the Temple of Rejuvenation experience, can you inform us now on what the approach to Temple wants to be as seen from above? Can you explain the ceremonial experience to us at this time?
    K. No more explanation as to the ceremony will be given (*see information given on pages 107 and 153*), except from your standpoint it is important to know that the ceremony begins and ends at the base of the legs. As channeled, there are different entrances for different participants. The most important leg is the one carrying the exit of the target human. This is seen almost as a "rebirth." The clothing worn by the target human is sacred, and is not removed for three days after the ceremony. Much celebration takes place with family and friends during this time. Therefore you can expect different metals and sculpture to be

used symbolically for each leg, representing its use. In addition there are facilities at the base of each leg to contain the ceremony for the participants, prior to and after the rejuvenation. Light, sound, and color were used well in these ceremonies. There was much appropriate emotion.

4. **M**. I see that at the top of the base structure, under the superstructure and within the circumference of the legs is a sunken courtyard open to the sky and Temple. The pool is very deep and appears to be illuminated, and becomes a whirlpool at times. When the pool is calm, the vertex of the lower spire nearly touches the surface of the water. Anything here?
    K. Yes Mark, the pool was there. The water is artificially illuminated to enhance what the bottom spire's engine does to it when in use, for within the process the magnetics are very strong. The energy, although well shielded, still is potent at the tip vortices of both spires. The top spire at the vertex dissipates it into the atmosphere, although there is a noticeable effect on the air during ceremony, one which you can see and smell just above and below the spires. The bottom spire's pool is meant to absorb and dissipate the effects of the engine's vortex. The vortex has the side effect of lifting and spinning the water slightly, as well as creating a beautiful mist. Again, light is used here in a magnificently beautiful manner. Humans are not allowed within 10 meters of the vortex.

Mark: It is a supreme honor and a pleasure to be given the opportunity to participate in the planning process. I am at your service and you are in my heart, as you have known.

$$\mathcal{Kryon}$$

Appendix B

Writer
Analysis of the Parables

Appendix B

From the writer...

The various parables given by Kryon have been a wonderful source of study for me. In this book there are four, and my favorite is the one that follows.

The definition of parable is that of a simple story to illustrate a lesson or moral. In the case of the Kryon parables, the story is simple, but often the entire meaning is waiting for further discovery and examination. Since we are in communication with Spirit during the giving of the parable, it would behoove us to glean all that we can from the message as given. Also, in this case I am the one who got to translate it, so there are fresh insights when I am able to revisit the channeling and give my interpretations.

Parable of The Room of Lesson (page 76)

I guess you all understand that the introduction of the character "Wo" by Kryon is an attempt at creating a non-gendered person. Wo is a Wo-man; which is it, woman or man? This is Spirit wishing not to create a gender slant to interfere with your full understanding of the parable, or your eventual ability to put yourself in the place of Wo.

Our language, like most, requires gender to speak normally, such as "he did this" or "she went there." Kryon then goes on to tell us that in this parable the "he" will be used for the purpose of language only. This is an important clue to the fact that when we are not on Earth, we are genderless; otherwise this distinction would not be so important. I bring this up for those who strongly feel that they might be "married as men and women in Heaven." I think the marriage is far different from the obvious partnering kind on Earth.

In the parable, Wo's house is obviously his life, or his "expression" (as Kryon calls a lifetime) on Earth. The analogy of the various rooms are in reference to the windows of opportunity that we all get, that come along with our contract, our karma, and therefore our potential.

Wo was obviously not directly troubled by living in a culture that had war or starvation. This relates to most of us reading this book, for this work is mainly channeled for those in the first world, as Kryon has told us. Therefore Wo is one of us. (Remember that Kryon has told us that there are 8 others channeling this information in various parts of the world, bringing messages to the other cultures). This is Spirit's invitation to put ourselves in the place of Wo for the story. If the parable had been about an individual beset by starvation and a war-ravaged economy, for instance, we would not relate at all.

The part about Wo learning what makes him happy, sad, and angry, and then hanging things on the wall to make him feel that way, is really insightful information about humans.

This refers to the parts of ourselves that dig into the past and revisit events in order to feel a certain way. Usually it's not appropriate enlightened behavior, since it dredges up old memories so that we can "feel" anger, hate, vindictiveness and victimization. Sometimes it's just good old wishing to be in a place that made us happy... like when we were growing up for instance.

The fact that Kryon said that Wo "placed things on the wall" for this purpose was also meaningful. When you come into my house, the items on the wall are for all to see. They are my family photos, and works of beauty. What this means is that I have placed things on the wall to give them emphasis, even for strangers that come in, because I feel the items are special. Therefore, Kryon has Wo hanging his feelings up for everyone to see and react to on his "wall" of lesson. Have you ever gone to visit people, only to sit through a sad story about how they are being mistreated, or how bad things are for them? Does this sound familiar, therefore, in the parable? Wo wants to involve others in his own process, since it makes him feel better to do so. Wo doesn't know about responsibility yet. Even so, later on we learn that no matter in what stage Wo is at in the enlightenment department,. there is no judgment about it... ever.

On page 77 we see that Wo has fears, and his main one is about control. It seems that in his life he fears the situations where someone could change his room (his life). His reaction to most of these fears is to **stay the same**. His real fear, therefore, is change, and he longs for stability, or a static awareness. He also feared the past, but he didn't know why (this is an obvious reference to the seed fear that Kryon speaks of regarding getting too close to real enlightenment).

He turns to other humans to learn about God, and he uses what he learns to *protect* him from change. This is a strong example of what religion is teaching today. We have God playing the role of responsible protector from evil, and the church members are encouraged to follow the shepherd's protection through the valley of the shadow of death. This hardly encourages empowering spiritual thought from individuals, or promotes the concept of taking responsibility for what happens to you.

The wonderful part of this story is that even though Wo "buys" into the average, normal kind of religious doctrine, he gets results from his prayers! He gets the protection he asks for, and he is indeed shielded from change, and from the disturbing motion in the corner. Again, Kryon has told us that the mechanics of Spirit are absolute, and that the loving energy of good prayerful intent gets results. Remember the adage "be careful what you ask for... you might get it"? It's true! This parable shows it.

Later we learn that Wo's house is huge, but by choice he stays in one room and dies there. This, of course, is referring to our full potential of contract when we arrive in any lifetime. This, depending on how much karma you dissolve, dictates the discovery of the important rooms. Although it wasn't mentioned in this parable, there are many "Wos" in the world who have many rooms, and are still not spiritually empowered. Each situation deals with the kind of karma you are working through. In Wo's case, his was fear of change, so he didn't venture about much in his "house."

We all get various chances for empowerment and self-discovery in every lifetime, and Wo got his. Even though he felt he had satisfactory answers, Spirit honored him with a "poke" from his guides. This was the irritating motion he saw in the corner, along with his vision of a door. It was his guide's efforts to bring him into another reality, thereby giving him his deserved opportunity for change... and a chance to face his fear. It was again insightful of Kryon to show what the religion of the day told him to do about it: Wo was told that the motion was the Devil (sigh). This is the most often quoted answer for anything contrary to popular selected doctrine. The religious leaders also asked Wo for money, and he was told that his reward would be a good future. Kryon has never referred to this before or since, but it has to do with the control that men have over those who turn to them for spiritual help.

So Wo finally died, and the thing he feared the most happened: the motion in the corner became reality. But he somehow recognized it and was not frightened. We go on to see the various rooms beyond the door, and share in Wo's discovery.

The room tour is an exposure of his contract, and along the way his potential enlightenment... with riches, peace, and personal inner essence of individual power, his "piece of God." He recognizes his guides along the way, showing us that we know who our guides really are, but have this hidden from us while we are here. Imagine going through life with two or three friends ready to help us and love us at every step... and ignoring them! Wo did this, and yet they did not stand in judgment of him. Such is the stuff that the love of Spirit is made of. Some of the other door names were really startling: I like the ones of unborn children. This is a direct reference to the fact that other entities could have come in to establish karmic interaction if Wo had let it happen, but in the parable Wo had no partner. This "potential children issue" requires prior planning. Think about it.

Another name on a door was "world leader," indicating that part of Wo's potential contract during this lifetime was to become politically involved, and become a leader. This is probably the last thing you would assign to the character of Wo, yet here it is! It's probably as remote a concept as a pragmatic businessman becoming a new-age channel in his late 40's (oh, well). Think about what Spirit was trying to tell us here: there is no limit to your imagination of what God has called you to do. If part of Wo's contract was to be a world leader, what do you think is behind your doors? This stuff should give you chills.

Wo began to get the picture and feel insecure that he had fouled up so badly. The guides, however, set him straight immediately and told him *"Do not be reproachful with your spirit, for it is inappropriate, and does not serve your magnificence."* This was Wo's crossover. He went at that moment from being a "past human in lesson" to becoming what he always was... a piece of God, a universal entity. The next thing he looked at was his real name on the door, and he remembered everything.

The most potent thing for me was contained in the last paragraphs of this parable. I repeat it here for easy reference:

"Wo knew the routine, for now He remembered everything, and He was no longer Wo. He said good-bye to his guides, and thanked them for their faithfulness. He stood for a long time looking at them, and loving them. Then He turned to walk toward the light at the end of the hallway. He had been here before. He knew what was waiting for him on his brief three-day trip to the cave of creation to retrieve his essence, and then on to the hall of honor and celebration, where those who loved him dearly were waiting for him, including those whom He had loved and lost while on Earth.

He knew where he had been, and where he was going.
Wo was going home."

Of course there is interesting information here, but not all that different from what we already have been given through the years. There is the light at the end of the tunnel that is described by "near-death experience" testimonials, and a three day trip to the cave of creation. I never knew it was three days, or what happens during that time. Perhaps more on this will be given later? Something entirely different affects me about this last section. It's a beautiful picture, but I was really there! Athough not contained in Chapter 11, this was a live channeled transcription, representing a session given before a group of people. When Kryon gives journeys and parables, he actually takes me there. In the case of his "journeys," I get to feel the wind and temperature, etc. This is why the flavor of these channelings are slightly different. Kryon often lets me describe what I am "seeing," in addition to his thought groups given to me for translation. In the process, however, I am affected greatly, often weeping with the joy of full understanding of what is being presented while I sit in my chair. There is nothing close to this in comparison, except what we get to feel in a very, very real dream.

I actually stood there as Wo did, poised at the brink of going home... bathed in Spirit. I felt the tug of love from those who were already there, and I longed for my friends. I saw my brilliant glowing guides (but did not see their faces), and felt their love, then I took the hand of Kryon and returned to my chair in the gathering in Del Mar.

Parable of The Farmer (page 110)

By now you can see that Kryon's parables are loaded with insightful attributes. Right off the bat we have two farmers. The farmer is used here to clearly represent a human in marriage with the Earth, toiling in harmony with nature to achieve life sustenance. Those of you who have followed the teaching of Kryon will relate to this very strong relationship of human to Earth, as has been channeled many times.

In addition, these farmers specifically were independent, able to "farm on their own, without help from others." So we have the setup of two humans walking the Earth who depend on the planet for sustenance, and who are totally responsible for everything around them. Does this scenario sound familiar? It's us, in a strong metaphor. So the farmers represent those of us walking the Earth right now.

The next part of the setup relates to those of us who live in relative security in the first world (as described before). Kryon exposes this when he states how the farmers lived good lives, and usually had good crops each year. This indicates the kind of life most of us have, where we work hard and generally make it somehow financially year to year. Kryon also goes on to expose that the parable takes place in a free economy, where "some of their harvest was used personally, and some was sold at market to provide sustenance and abundance." These words are all important, for they place the story firmly within our free economic society.

The biggest exposure, however, is this sentence: "One day a human appeared in each of their fields, claiming to have a message from God. Both farmers were interested, and listened intently to the message." This is an amazing clue to whom Kryon is actually speaking of as the principles in the parable! What would happen with most folks if a fellow showed up telling them that he had a message from God? Most would throw the guy out and have a good laugh (such is the culture we live in). But these farmers were different, because they "were interested, and listened intently to the message." Note that they were not just passively interested, but listened intently. Most of you reading this are seeing where this is going... and what Kryon means is that he is about to give us a parable about two humans living in the new age who are **enlightened**. Hopefully, this will include most of you reading these words, for the practical part of me says that this is the kind of person who bought this book.

This is not the first time that Kryon has spoken directly to the ones who have discovered their higher selves, and this is a parable especially for them. I suspect it's especially for you.

The parable goes on to describe how the messenger lets them know that they have a reward coming, but in order to take it, they have to do something different and illogical. It's something they have not done before, and goes against what they have been taught works for agriculture (in other words, don't think like a human if you want your reward).

Look closely at what they were told: The basic translation is (1) *Purge the old crop* – Get rid of all your past ways of doing things. (2) *Plow it under* – Bury your past ways so completely that they are truly gone. (3) *Cast out the impurities and parasites as you plow it back under* – Don't keep attachments around, including things in your life that you have always had riding along, but that you have intuitively known are wrong for you. (4) *Reseed immediately* – Start growing with the new energy, and the new ways of things right now.

(5) The messenger then went on to let them know that the Earth around them was going to change, allowing this new arrangement to be comfortable and support them. This, of course, is the Kryon message: that the Earth's grid is changing to allow for the new energy, and for the "passing of the torch," so to speak, to all humans on this planet of free choice. We are being told to embrace the new energy, get used to it, and that the Earth will cooperate and marry to all of it in support of us.

As the story goes on, one farmer has big trouble with all of this, since his crop is ready to harvest, and he really doesn't believe everything he was told by the messenger. Kryon tells us that both farmers were hesitant to destroy a full crop, showing that it was even difficult for the one who finally did as he was advised. This means that what is being asked of us is hard! It won't be easy for any of us to truly cast out the old ways we do things, and embrace the new energy. Even with vast rewards promised (like extended life), it's hard, since we can't really see what is ahead.

Still, I always wondered in the parable how a messenger from God could be ignored. Then I chuckled to myself when I remembered that in Sunday school I asked myself the same question when I first learned about Pharaoh hardening his heart time after time, when Moses kept bringing "big time" proof that it was bad news not to let the slaves go. Was Pharaoh stupid or what? Now Kryon is showing me the same "hard streak" in us all! It's really difficult to change our ways when they are so dear to us, and we have depended on them for so long.

In the parable one farmer follows the advice and the other does not. Shortly thereafter both are shocked at Earth changes (rains and winds come that never had before at that seasonal time). As the story goes, the Earth changes are beneficial to the farmer's crop who had followed the messenger's advice, and indeed his newly seeded crop grows to record heights. The other farmer's crop is destroyed (even though it was healthy and tall).

The admonition here is clear: the old ways will no longer work. The Earth changes are going to make them fall on barren ground, and they will no longer grow. Even the most healthy and successful old energy methods are going to fall away. The ones that will be successful are new, often different, and represent uncharted waters. They are also the methods that will be filled with love, abundance, and results.

This parable was directly for the enlightened, the teachers and the workers. It was given in the middle of 1993, and amazing validations of this have come forward, showing that this parable was not to be taken lightly. Take a moment to read it again. It's short, but packed with a wonderful message.

As for the human messenger in the story... you figure it out.

Parable of The Tar Pit (page 123)

Take a look at this one paragraph parable that contains some of the most clear answers about the workings of the neutral implant. In this parable Kryon has humans in a tar pit "covered with tar, dirty from head to foot, unable to move quickly from place to place because the tar is thick."

This is us in normal life in the old energy, chained by old karmic lessons, and walking the best we can carrying it all around with us. Kryon then gives five words that are part of his cosmic humor. He says, "This is your imagined state." This is Kryon's way of reminding us all that the Earth experience is not reality, and that our duality is a phantom. The real Universe is what we experience when we are not here.

In the parable the "magic tool from God" is the implant. Suddenly as you receive the implant, the tar no longer sticks to you, and you walk around unencumbered and clean. This is a strong reference to how the implant affects you (as has been channeled by Kryon since 1992). You are no longer held to karmic contracts, and can move forward on the planet toward a marriage with your higher self, and eventual ascension (graduate) status. Kryon also casually mentions that we have "co-created" the magic tool. Wait a minute! I thought the magic tool was from God, you might say. Again, Kryon wants us to remember that he calls us "pieces of God, walking the Earth in lesson." In other words, we are God.

Next, he has us walking around in this state without the tar touching us, indicating that not only has our karma been dispersed, but also the karmic ties with those who had the opportunity to interact with ours. This, of course, is the object of the parable, to show how our decision creates changes on a larger scale than just for us.

He goes on to describe what happens to those around us. This is really important, and I hope you as the reader can not only "get" this, but have the ability to explain it to others, for it is a constant question about the implant.

Will we lose our mates, our kids, our jobs, etc., if we take the implant? Will we be outcasts? Listen to what the parable says: "Do you think the others around you will ignore you as you walk freely without the tar touching you or encumbering your feet?" The first thing is that everyone will notice that you are different, but instead of casting you out, the opposite potential exists. Others will look at how you are living, and respond. Some will want the same thing and ask about what happened to you, and some will just be glad that you changed. As far as mates and kids, they will see it first, and be most puzzled what has taken place to make you such a swell balanced person all of a sudden!

When you balance a person spiritually, physically and mentally, a funny thing happens: everyone wants to be your friend! They recognize the specialness of who you are, and are not threatened by you in any way. Can you see how this would enhance a job, a marriage, a friendship, or a generation gap (and not destroy it)? The only ones you will offend are those who are angry that you've changed... and believe me folks, those are the ones you don't want around you anyway.

When it is all said and done, even though you might be the only one who takes the implant, dozens around you will be affected by your choice. This is part of the way Spirit uses individual choices of humans to create energy that will benefit many. Perhaps you can see the dynamics of this, and truly understand how the implant is far more important than it appears.

Parable of Angenon & Veréhoo (page 178)

Just when I thought we were finished with Wo (page 76), he's back! But this time he is a *she*, and the entire story is told from the perspective of the guides this time.

This parable contains important information regarding the working of the guides. Remember that in earlier writings Kryon has told us of the fact that we all come in with at least two guides who are with us always, and that some of us get a third; and that with the implant there is the potential of a full guide change. This full guide change is the 90-day depression he speaks of in Book One.

Right away Kryon lets us know about the two guides who are going to be assigned to "Wo." I have no idea about the significance of the guide names Angenon & Veréhoo. Perhaps there are those reading this who have some validation of what these names might indicate, and would like to write me with your ideas? I put an accent mark on Veréhoo, since it was given to me as VER (sounds like 'fur')-A (as in 'hay')-HOO (sounds like 'who').

One guide has been human, and one has not. This information would indicate that humans don't always come back as humans. Did you ever wonder if your "guardian angel" was someone you used to know? This is evidence that it actually could be that way! Anyway, the information is that the guides are specialists in service to support us in lesson, and that the guide group contains those who were always guides, and others who were humans... and whatever else that we don't know about right now.

The next bit of information is that the guides are with us when the contracts are planned. Kryon has told us from the start that we are God. That we, while in God consciousness (something that humans can't understand fully), plan our own incarnations and the lesson opportunities within them. This, by the way, makes us totally responsible for absolutely everything that happens to us along the way, since Spirit has let us know through countless channels that "there are no accidents," and that "coincidence" isn't.

So the guides are going to the planning meeting to meet the human they will accompany, and actually plan the opportunities for the next life! This is wonderful information, and helps us to understand why the guides are important... for they stand by to implement plans that we all helped make.

Here we also hear of the "cave of creation" again: "*Wo stands now in the chamber of planning, close to the portal leading to the cave of creation.*" If you are curious about what this cave is (like I was), there is information on page 68. Also, when Kryon uses the word "portal," it can be anywhere in the Universe. This word means a gate to somewhere else.

Kryon also wants us again to recognize the difference between what is going on in this planning session in regard to predestination. Predestination is a human concept and is not a reality with Spirit. Our planning sessions are only setups of lesson. In other words, when you are in school at your desk, you can do anything you want with the test in front of you: throw it away, make a paper airplane and fly it out the window, or pass it! It's totally up to you. In this case, the test was written by you when you were in a "God consciousness," but you don't recognize this fact at all. Can you see how this differs greatly from predestination? We have total free choice all the time. Kryon's humor shows here where a few paragraphs later he again gives an example about predestination: "*If you were to send entities down to Earth as hammers, and visited them some years later, you would not be surprised to find them in the company of nails.*" This is his way of presenting the logic of the planning to our human minds. In this imaginary setting, we set up the hammer entities, but didn't "make them" find nails. They did it by choice, since it was only logical.

The next piece of startling information is that the planning session includes the *"higher souls of those already on Earth walking in lesson."* Take a look at this! It's the first indication from Kryon that karmic planning involves those already living and walking around. This is how the "engine" of group karma is therefore facilitated. In other words, if Spirit always had to wait for humans to pass on before the next incarnations were planned, it would be very inefficient. Entities would be literally "standing around" waiting for the others to die before they could plan how to interact with them the next time. Think about it: you interact karmically with parents and children; therefore, there are big age differences. This, therefore, is how it can be that a child could come into the world, die appropriately for the lesson of the parents, and then come in again shortly thereafter as still another child of the same parents (if appropriate). I say this not to indicate that Spirit has this scenario happen, but to show how the communication works.

How can the planning involve the living, you might ask? Kryon has told us on many occasions of the "oversoul" or "higher self" of each of us. In fact, the quest of the implant and ascension is to marry to your higher self and stick around the planet as a power worker. Evidently this higher self is part of us, in contact with Spirit all the time, but whose energy is not totally in our bodies (again see page 68). Therefore, there is still communication with Spirit on karmic things (at least). This also helps explain how the complex interactions of karma can continue to change as those around us work through their karma, and we work through ours. In other words, we alter the lesson plan as we pass each test. Part of us is keeping score!

The story goes on to have Wo incarnate on the first of September as a woman. Those of you knowledgeable in Astrology will understand when Kryon says the words, "She is going to have a difficult time with control."

The story sets up Wo as an abused child who is abused by many men who are supposed to be her family support group. This is given to help you see how the abandonment karma is set up, and what kind of personality type might result. Remember, Kryon is a master of human psychology, since the very grid system we live in is his domain, and is associated very strongly with our biology.

Evidently Wo becomes an overachiever woman with no problem with money, but a lot of trouble with men. (No wonder!) She likes to win at business, and enjoys the competition with men (the actual translation was that she liked to beat them at their own game). She has three failed marriages or relationships of some kind, and carries around a great deal of anger, which later gives her an ulcer and other stress-related problems.

Now where were Angenon and Veréhoo all this time? What good is all this guardian angel stuff if they don't do anything to help this mess? Well, these questions are joke questions, since the reality is that *"Angenon and Veréhoo watched in love, quietly knowing that all was appropriately set for the next stage..."* All 47 years of this woman's life were a setup to a great test that was coming. Think of it... the patience of the guides!

Now I have to stop here to reflect on my own experience, and again let you know that I was in my mid-forties when Kryon came along. If I had believed in Astrology, I would have known something was up, for my chart targeted something very special at this time (I found out later). This is the way the old energy of Earth worked. I have to let you younger folks know that time is now of the essence, and that Spirit won't keep you around 40 years while you mark time (like I did). The new energy is far different now, and promotes intent immediately. Even those under 20 reading this book, who relate to what is presented here, will know intuitively that their contract will start bringing enlightenment instantly with intent. Our time is speeding up, in a universal sense, and Spirit is working with us faster and earlier than ever before. Don't be put off by this story of how Wo had to wait 47 years.

Now, back to the story. The "scheduled one" arrived on the scene. The guides recognized her instantly and got excited. Reading on, this scheduled person that came into Wo's life was actually part of the contract planning session 47 years earlier. Think of the complexity of this! In her own way Wo recognized the woman also, because it says that Wo was interested in her and the things she had to say. Here was a woman who was different: the tar wasn't sticking to her! (You'd better go back and read the last parable analysis if you don't understand this.) Look how the parables intertwine with the same information: here is an enlightened woman who comes into Wo's life and causes Wo to change!... and all she has to do is be there.

So it goes that Wo had to know about this unnamed woman's peace and inner joy... and her tolerance toward men. Remember that Wo was now in a state of imbalance and was ill. This was the state necessary for her to surrender enough of her ego to ask another woman about these intangible things. Notice also how the parable used a woman to be the messenger for this other woman, even though we are all humans, and our gender isn't supposed to make a difference to Spirit. It does when karma is concerned, for much of the karma we carry is the energy generated around the opposite sex (father and mother issues, etc.). Science lately has also discovered that our brains are biologically connected differently, and it has finally acknowledged that we actually think differently. (No kidding! I wonder how much money they spent on that? I could have verified it for nothing, had they asked.)

The woman shared the truth of Spirit with Wo. The guides were poised and ready for this event. Here was the test they had expected and waited for. The parable tells us that Wo asked for help alone in her room, and by verbalizing her intent, she started the amazing process that followed.

The story goes on to tell of the changes in Wo's life, and of the third guide that joined Angenon and Veréhoo down the line. This guide was from a "master guide group." Again, Kryon speaks of the master guides as being different from the normal ones. To some, this is the same as receiving a higher kind of angel in their lives. All this nomenclature is appropriate, since my translation of Kryon uses only my words. I believe that one could use the words "guides or angels" interchangeably if desired, and that it really isn't important what you call them, as long as you understand the incredible mechanics of why they are here, and the love they carry for us.

Wo ended up being an enlightened human... forgiving those in her past, recognizing that she was responsible for everything, and having peace, finally having real peace. At that point she was able to partner with a man and make it work... the real test.

Look at what happens next: our heroes Angenon and Veréhoo are replaced! What kind of story is this anyway, where the good guys get replaced in the middle? This would never work in the movies. How do you think Angenon and Veréhoo felt? Weren't they good enough to stay with Wo from here on? After all, they had endured 47 years of anger and frustration! Hadn't they earned a chance to stay on and enjoy the results of the planning they had helped with?

Wo had taken the implant, and was moving toward a status which demanded master guides, and Angenon and Veréhoo knew it and were ecstatic with joy. They departed with much love and no sadness. They had been part of Earth history, and celebrated all of it.

Such is the mind of Spirit that one entity can celebrate the joy of the other so completely. Once you truly see the big picture, you can celebrate your neighbor's good fortune, and mean it, even if you are feeling that your life isn't going as well as his. Some folks never understand how this can be. Putting on the "Mantle of Spirit" is what Kryon asks us to do. This means to carry with us the connection to the higher self, and move into such balance that our first feelings toward all humans is love-based, without all the other baggage that used to be dragged in. Honor the one next to you, for his process is related to yours, even if you feel it is vastly different.

Offered in Love,

The Writer

If you have enlightenment and know what is happening, and wish to be part of the great plan, it is not our desire that you be crushed by a boulder or drowned by a flood. We wish you to stay. Reach out to your guides this very night, and take their hands!

(page 201 - Live session "Your Wake Up Call")

Appendix
C

More on Magnetics

Appendix C

From the writer...

Aren't you glad you are reading the Appendix? Usually it's pretty dry stuff, but in this case our Appendix contains some valuable information and insight into the work of Kryon. This Appendix is no exception.

I have to make a "cutoff" point for this book somewhere, knowing full well that the newest information from Kryon must be put off to Book Three. Even as I write this, I am only weeks away from giving this book to the printer. However, I feel I am compelled again to bring you some new information, and a review of some dangers of everyday magnetics.

In May 94 Kryon gave an important live session before a group in Del Mar. Del Mar was the "home room" for Kryon, but this was the last live event for the area, since we were going to travel and take the live channeling work on the road. This would allow some of the rest of the cities to experience the energy of Kryon first hand... and also to bring some very special people into the influence of Kryon's healing power, to fulfill their contracts. (This may sound like weird stuff, but it was part of my instructions.) There is an agenda here that I only find out about as I go along day to day (sigh).

An interesting thing about this particular last light group was that it did not get recorded. The digital machine that we were using to record all light groups ate the tape! Since there are "no accidents," I presumed that Kryon wanted the information to be for only those attending... making it an evening that was special indeed for those 115 people.

During the channeling, however, Kryon spoke of some new magnetic information which I will recap at this time. The subject was the exposure of whole cells to magnetic fields. Kryon said that magnetic fields affect whole cells directly, but that in order to study the phenomenon, science should expose individual cells to a "focused" field (and not a stray one), then look for secretions from the cells in direct response to the magnetic stimulus. His challenge to scientists was to find this correlation, so that all would know about it.

Before I define what Kryon meant by focused fields, let me tell you also the "why" involved in this correlation. Hard to prove, but channeled just the same, was the Kryon information that part of the DNA system consists of invisible magnetic strands that provide the magnetic information to each cell. This magnetic information helps the cells to know what their purpose is (the difference of an "ear" cell from a "toe" cell for instance), as well as each cell's "regeneration properties." (Did you ever wonder why your liver can regenerate completely, as well as your skin, but you can't grow a new hand?) This new information also helps to explain why some are convinced that we have more DNA strands coming to complete our "ageless body" ascended forms. If some of these strands are invisible, or non biological, then we already have some of them in place! Remember... our title Don't Think Like a Human reminds us that it is a poor human assumption that all the DNA strands are just like the others, and have to be biological.

This magnetic DNA information is the new source of science for the Temple of Rejuvenation (TOR), which Kryon has spoken of often, and which occupies other parts of this book, and Appendix A. Evidently Kryon invites us to revisit the science of altering this DNA magnetic stripe through the TOR process, thereby creating a very long life by balancing our biology, and giving it instructions (via the magnetic strands) to regenerate more often! At last we have the "tie in" as to the cellular mechanics that the TOR engine provides us to live longer (see pages 107, 153, 160, and Appendix A for more Temple information).

Kryon speaks of the fact that the cells are addressed directly by the magnetic strands, and that the magnetics involved act like a code for the cells. This handshakes very nicely with the biological DNA which also acts like a code. In fact, DNA is very much like computer programming code, complete with stop and start sequences of amino acids which identify the beginning and end of instruction sets for the proteins. Quite a system!

According to Kryon, certain magnetic fields can have an effect on individual cells, and **unlike the effects of radiation** (which causes damage or unusual growth), science should look for the cells to react as though they were receiving biological instructions, since they will actually **secrete chemicals** in direct response to magnetic stimulation of focused fields. The main point of this channeling was that our biology doesn't just react to any magnetic field... but a certain kind. If our cells are used to reacting to specific polarized designed magnetics that give instructions, then they will tend to react to other designed symmetrical fields, as though these were also instructions. The stray magnetics fields, although strong, might do nothing at all to the cells.

The difference between stray and focused fields isn't all that hard to explain. A magnetic focused field is any magnetic field that is designed. This is what Kryon meant by "focused." Here are some examples: A simple magnet is a designed field. It has symmetrical lines of influence and a known strength which is constant. It therefore would be a very nice tool for a lab study. An electromagnet is even better, since it has everything the magnet has, plus the ability to vary the intensity of the field. A good experiment, therefore, would be to place identical kinds of live cells separately in the positive and negative influence of such a field at various intensities, and look specifically for cells to secrete some chemical in direct response to the magnetic stimulus. Also, if I were doing the experiment, I would place some cells midway between the positive and negative poles as well. Naturally the control would be a group of similar cells placed in an area of no magnetics at all.

Other examples of designed fields that wouldn't be good for the lab, but that are with us daily nevertheless, are (1) Electric blankets. Electric blankets are not designed to create magnetic fields, but they create designed fields anyway due to their consistency of coiled wiring with electricity flowing through it. (Remember from science class 1A, that even a single wire with current flowing through it can produce a magnetic field of some kind.) (2) Electric motors are another example of designed fields. Motors create strong fields, even though the purpose of the motor is as an electric engine. The field is only a by-product, but a "designed" one, since it mirrors the design of the motor. A hair dryer is a good example of a strong field created by a motor in everyday life. (3) Static magnets for stereo speakers are also a hidden source. These are just magnets, and therefore are designed fields. If you want to know how deceivingly strong these are, just get a normal cheap compass and see how close you can get to your speakers at home before they move the needle. You may be surprised at how far away from the speaker you are when the needle swings. Remember: if it can swing a compass needle, it can affect you! (4) Another designed and dangerous source is a neighborhood transformer box. (It's the green thing about the size of a US mail box that is usually mounted on a cement slab around some bushes... and hums.) There often is one of these for every few houses in newer neighborhoods. As long as they are on the street, you are okay, but I have seen them put right next to houses on occasion. These are definitely bad to have close to your living quarters. (5) Finally, your computer monitor (if not the newer shielded kind) may produce ELF (extremely low frequency) magnetic fields. This field is symmetrical, designed, and can affect your biology. My thanks personally go to the many consumer computer magazines that exposed this potential hazard, and actually got the manufacturers to do something about it **before there was proof that it was a problem**. Public perception can change things! Perhaps even this book can make a difference?

Stray fields are unorganized, non-designed fields. A good example of this would be power lines. In this case, the fields generated are not symmetrical due to the fact that there are so many smaller fields interacting with each other (some cancel each other out). Also, the current through the wires changes all the time, making the intensity and the symmetry of any field change constantly. It's really a "pot luck" deal if power lines are aligning magnetically to bring about a focused field, since some scenarios might not ever "come together" in an organized way. In other cases, the situation might be "just right" randomly to create a strong field with consistent symmetry, thereby nicely emulating a designed field. In this case you have a real problem, since the field strength potential is so high. So we should treat power lines as though they could always be a problem, even though not all are. This is why a scientific study of power lines on health is such a difficult thing. Power lines in themselves are not the problem. It's the random organization of the magnetic field that is the important attribute. It's no wonder that conclusive evidence isn't at hand. You might have some "killer" power lines at one house, and down the street another identical looking pole could be benign. The real way to show the planet that there is a health danger is to provide evidence that controlled magnetic fields affect human cells! Then prove that there are magnetic fields around certain power lines on an individual case-by-case basis. The rest is just logic.

Another example of an unorganized field would be from those created by your house's electric junction box (usually where your meters are located). Many times this junction is responsible for some stray magnetics, but usually it is random and non-focused, and therefore often too unorganized to be of concern. It has the potential for harm, however, just like the power lines do.

The bottom line is to stay cognizant of all fields, designed and undesigned. Really go out of your way not to live daily next to the known designed ones. Here is a review of examples: Don't have large stereo speakers next to your bed. Use your compass to check this. Don't use an electric blanket! This is by far the worst offender. Imagine spending 8 hours a night in a designed field? Use a hair dryer only if you must, and then no longer than necessary. That motor next to your head is really powerful. Again, use a compass to verify this. You might be surprised at the fact that the motor itself has a static magnetic field that is fairly powerful, even without being turned on. So store the thing in a drawer that isn't next to your bed pillow. Be aware that all electric motors are strong creators of magnetic fields. Don't sleep with a fan next to your head. Use the "3 meter rule" to be safe, as stated in Kryon Book One.

There are also some systems of designed fields you can buy today that are supposed to "marry" to your biology and actually help tune up your cells. There are even some you can get to sleep on (made in Europe and Asia). I cannot possibly pass judgment on any of these. Use your intuition! If you purchase one of these systems, get it on a trial basis. Your body will scream at you if it isn't right; but the main point here is if you are connected enough to the workings of your biology to "hear it scream." The answer again is INTENT. Take time to meditate, and let your precious biology know you love it and honor it. Then ask it for help, and proceed. It won't fail you!

In love,   The Writer

Would you like to be on the Kryon mailing list?

This list is used to inform interested people of Kryon workshops coming to their areas, new Kryon releases, and Kryon news in general. We don't sell or distribute our lists to anyone.

If you would like to be included, please simply drop a post card to us that says "LIST," and include your clearly printed name and address.

The Kryon Writings

1155 Camino Del Mar – #422
Del Mar, California 92014

Appendix
D

More About The Dark Ones

Appendix D

From the writer...

So! Some of you turned to this page right away (go ahead, admit it). Everyone is curious about the dark ones. Some of you are calling them the "greys," the "Zeta," or "lizzies." Kryon channeled a very informative and loving message in January 1994 entitled "The Only Planet of Free Choice." In that discussion was a section on the Zeta. Since it will be some time before Book III is complete, I have enclosed this information now:

Kryon Channel 1/94

Now I will speak to you about something else which is taking place, both offered as admonishment and proof at the same time. I will now clear some of the information about previously channeled entities you call the Dark Ones.

We want you to understand, and realize, that the Dark Ones are not dark at all. The Dark Ones, who poke and prod you, and who are here to interface with you, are simply of another polarity. You see, they do not have Love. And so to you, many of them are frightening, and their ways are frightening. For some of them simply take from you, and do not ask.

Although I have spoken of many kinds of Dark Ones, I would like to be more specific about the ones whom you would call "The Zeta." Here is channeled information for you regarding these. There are many kinds of Zeta, for it is a fragmented society. You see them as dark, but they are simply without Love. They are here for one purpose only: they are curious about Love, and they desperately want the emotions that you so freely use.

Some of them have come in to communicate with you, and some of them come to you and create fear. There have been those who have entered the bodies of some of you, only to be perceived as "evil spirits," creating imbalance (the imbalance is perceived by other humans as the possession of an evil spirit).

Some of them come in another dimension, and will actually abduct your spirit... deal with you, ask you questions, and return you to the Earth. This is very unsettling, very uncentering. *When they do this*, some of them will ask and some of them will not. They cannot even agree among themselves what is appropriate. Some of them do not even communicate with each other... such is their fragmented society. How should you treat this? How can I prove to you that something unusual is taking place on Earth involving the Zeta? Here is the proof:

Dear Ones, go back in your records and see what has transpired since 1985 regarding the Zeta. You see, they also are Universal Entities, so they're aware of Earth being the only planet of free choice. They are very, very intellectual, and have great intelligence and logic. They knew of the *Earth's* interrogation in 1987, and started their campaign early to channel information to you, so that you would be accustomed to them and listen to their logic. Why else would they suddenly have such a visible presence (*showing themselves through channeling in the last few years*), unless they understood the timing of your planet? *They have been here a very long time. Why should they suddenly start communicating in the last 10 years?*

You see, they are afraid of losing you. Why would they fear this? Because this is the planet of **Free Choice** (*and you are just becoming aware of it*). What I am saying to you is this: if any of you are dealing with these entities, you have the **choice** to remain dealing with them or not, as you choose. This is the truth,

regardless of what they may tell you. The information that they give you, although it is channeled accurately, is purposefully not truthful from the Zeta. For they would have you believe that there is an agreement whereby you <u>must</u> help them. They would have you believe that there is an agreement where you have no choice. This is not so. *It is your choice to let them in or not, but the fear they create keeps you from seeing this. Now they are trying the intellectual approach with those of you who are starting to awaken to the truth.*

If you find yourself in a position where they are causing imbalance in your life, simply tell them to go away! They must. You are in control. This is the planet of Free Choice. They must retreat. But Dear Ones, there is also an appropriateness for those of you who wish to help them, for you may do so if you desire. You must interrogate the Zeta first, and request them to ask your permission!

This is what will help the Dark Ones the most: for them to realize *who you are*, and shout: **Honor!** It is part of their lesson. You see, their being here is like karma, and they have permission to be here. They have permission to ask you things, to prod and to poke, just as karma has permission to be here, so that you will walk through the lessons of appropriateness, and have the things happen in your lives that you must deal with to raise the vibration of the planet. So the Dark Ones are a part of this scheme. They dress up *seemingly* with frightening masks in your lives to create fear. This has been their way; for to create fear gets results... and they know this.

Dear Ones, the first emotion you might give them, if you choose, is fear, and they will feed on it. Instead, why not give them Love? *With love will come power!* Ask them to retreat, and they will do so... or demand that they ask your permission, and see what happens.

Kryon

From the writer... about the dark ones.

I was also curious about the dark ones, and after this channeling I wanted to know even more. For instance, is Kryon speaking about the "Lizzies," or the Zeta "Greys?" He told me that he was speaking about both (but he singled out the Zeta). Both kinds have something in common with each other: They both are here to probe us for our emotional side. (Interesting huh?)

In case you didn't get the message, Kryon says that they are lying to us. (Is that clear enough?). Humans who are channeling them are in integrity within the translations, but the Zeta are clever, and are trying to have us believe that we must comply with them due to some kind of prior universal commitment. So they are giving false information to be translated.

When Kryon offers proof of their skullduggery, it comes in the logical form of their actions since 1985. They know that we are beginning to get the picture, and that soon we will simply say "no" to their being here. Rather than let that happen, they have really been stepping up the communications (take a look at the books that are out there already) to involve our participation. I feel they are almost in a panic.

Now, that's all well and good, but how do we say "no" when many of these beings are not in our dimension (all the way at least), and can seemingly snatch us when we are "asleep"? The answer is to practice "lucid dreaming." I didn't make this up; the term is scientific. This is where we practice controlling our dreams to the degree that we can choose to take control within them, or wake up. Some of you have become so good at this that you can move freely within the scope of any dream, speaking, moving about, and deciding if you want the dream at all! (Talk about virtual reality... wow!)

By practicing lucid dreaming, we can firmly take control of a situation where we are faced with the fear of abduction while apparently sleeping. For those of you who have had experiences that were very real and fearful while you were awake or asleep, Kryon says that you have the power and permission to take the direct approach and just say "no." This requires that you take your power, and do some serious work on yourselves to integrate your body with Spirit.... which is the subject of this entire book. Without the integration, you will remain powerless before them; such are the mechanics of fear.

I really didn't mean for these to be the last words in this book, but it just turned out that way. Again I would like to encourage any of you who have gone through the implant process, and can describe your experiences, to write about it to me. I would like a portion of Book Three to be filled with testimonies about what it was like, and how it affected not only you, but the people around you. Many have written asking for this kind of information, and I feel that the readers of Books One and Two may actually end up writing parts of Book Three!

Finally, the answer to a trivial question. How is it that Book One was 168 pages for $12, and Book Two is 288 pages for the same price? When self-publishing, you have control over everything: the price, the marketing, the cover, etc., etc. Book One was originally printed in small quantities, since we had no idea what the response would be. The smaller quantity set the price, which couldn't easily be changed later. Book Two was printed in a larger quantity, allowing for the price to be lower; so I passed the savings along to you. What a concept.

In love,

Index

Products

Kryon Book One
The End Times
ISBN 0-9636304-2-3
$12 + S&H

Kryon Book Three
Alchemy of The Human Spirit
ISBN 0-9636304-8-2
$14 + S&H

Kryon Book Two
Don't Think Like a Human!
ISBN 0-9636304-0-7
$12 + S&H

The Kryon Tapes

EARTH CHANGES – $10
Original live channeling about MYRVA the "death rock" on its way to Earth (a fact verified in this book!) and what Kryon had to do with it during the three years prior to his coming to the planet. Good news indeed!

PAST LIVES, PRESENT FEARS – $10
Recreated past life experiences highlight this channeling as Kryon takes the audience on multiple journeys of the most significant past deaths of some of the more than 100 in attendance... quite real!

CHANGES WITHIN YOU – $10
Your questions about the implant are discussed. Is it for you? Join Kryon as he explores this issue, and also reveals some startling information regarding certain young people on the planet in this New Age.

HONORING THE PLANET OF FREE CHOICE – $10
Original live channeling that challenged Earth scientists to observe the incoming gamma bursts!... Later verified by mainstream science (Kryon Book II). Marvelous information regarding our place in the Universe.

ASCENSION & THE NEW AGE – $10 *(Chapter 8 in Kryon Book III - live!)*
We hear Jan's guided meditation, then Kryon speaks of the popular subject of ascension. Can we achieve it? Is it something we should be preparing for? Kryon also gives good advice for what to do after receiving the implant. Action is needed to activate it!

CRYSTAL SINGER – $12
Outstanding musical tape offered by Jan Tober, Kryon co-worker and vocalist (Stan Kenton & Benny Goodman tours). Jan offers two personal 17-minute healing meditations with channeled vocals and soothing instrumentals... very powerful and effective for daily use! (We get letters.)

Books and tapes can be purchased in retail stores,
or by phone - Credit cards welcome.
(800) 352-6657